Explaining *Guanxi*

Guanxi, a system of Chinese business relationships, is often described but is rarely fully understood. Translated loosely as 'personal ties', this simple explanation belies a complex and nuanced system.

This insightful book provides a much-needed explanation of the phenomena as it relates to business. It investigates:

- why it was initiated and developed
- what function it serves
- how it is maintained
- why it is such a dominant phenomenon in Chinese business life.

Drawing on cultural, organizational and economic studies, the book takes a multi-disciplinary approach, integrating these various topics into a coherent explanation of why *guanxi* came into being, why it continues to flourish and what its future holds. Clear and concise, this illuminating book will be equally useful to students of Asian business as to practitioners working within this market.

Ying Lun So obtained his BSocSc in 1982 at the University of Hong Kong. Subsequently he obtained an MBA at the Chinese University of Hong Kong and his PhD from the University of Hong Kong. His research interests include the economic analysis of *guanxi*, the relationship between Chinese culture and business practices, institutional arrangements and business strategies.

Anthony Walker is Professor Emeritus in Real Estate and Construction at the University of Hong Kong. His major research area is project management in construction and he has published extensively on this topic and on the real estate and construction business in China generally and Hong Kong specifically.

Explaining *Guanxi*

The Chinese business network

Ying Lun So and Anthony Walker

Routledge
Taylor & Francis Group

LONDON AND NEW YORK

First published 2006
by Routledge
2 Park Square, Milton Park, Abingdon, Oxon OX14 4RN

Simultaneously published in the USA and Canada
by Routledge
270 Madison Ave, New York, NY 10016

Routledge is an imprint of the Taylor & Francis Group

© 2006 Ying Lun So and Anthony Walker

Typeset in Charter by
Keystroke, Jacaranda Lodge, Wolverhampton
Printed and bound in Great Britain by
MPG Books Ltd, Bodmin

British Library Cataloguing in Publication Data
A catalogue record for this book is available from the British Library

Library of Congress Cataloging in Publication Data
So, Ying Lun.
Explaining guanxi : the Chinese business network / Ying Lun So and
Anthony Walker
p. cm.
Includes bibliographical references and index.
1. Business networks–China. 2. Interorganizational relations–China.
3. Interpersonal relations–China. 4. Corporate culture–China.
5. Industrial sociology–China. I. Walker, Anthony, 1939– II. Title.
HD69.S8S66 2006
658′.044–dc22
2005015107

ISBN10: 0–415–38417–6   ISBN13: 9–78–0–415–38417–9 (hbk)
ISBN10: 0–415–38418–4   ISBN13: 9–78–0–415–38418–6 (pbk)

To our wives, Clio and Pam

Contents

Preface

China's economic development is no longer front-page news although specific spectacular advances continue to startle the business community, politicians and the world at large. With China set to become the world's second largest economy in the first quarter of the twenty-first century much attention has been focused on how the Chinese do business. But Chinese entrepreneurship is not new. China has been doing business for centuries and the Chinese diaspora has built business communities in many countries. A common characteristic of these economic activities has been the Chinese business networks – or *guanxi*.

Guanxi is clearly recognized by Chinese people as a powerful aid to business and is also widely acknowledged by non-Chinese businessmen and investors as something they must understand and deal with when handling Chinese businesses. Whilst the Chinese understand how *guanxi* operates in practice, both strategically and in its minutia, non-Chinese are likely to have only a broad idea of how it works. However what they have in common is a lack of understanding of why and how *guanxi* came into being in the first place. Knowing the origins of *guanxi* is a great help in understanding how it works in practice and is of equal value to both Chinese and non-Chinese.

The roots of this explanation lie in economics, law and culture and require an academic approach that synthesizes the relevant parts of these disciplines in a multi-faceted analysis. Much has been written about the operation of *guanxi* in practice but this is not the purpose of this book, rather it offers an original view of *guanxi's* historical development, from which emerges understanding.

Our partnership in writing the book was formed in Hong Kong, the perfect place for East–West collaboration. The Eastern side (Y.L. So) felt the need to explain the historical aspects of *guanxi*, which has been passed down the generations for thousands of years, through an analysis based on modern economic thinking. The Western side (Tony Walker) encouraged the Eastern side to reach a wider audience by adapting the text to appeal to academics from a wide range of disciplines and to managers and businessmen, both Chinese and non-Chinese.

The authors hope that their book makes some contribution to a greater understanding of Chinese society and the manner by which the academic disciplines of economics, law and culture can aid that understanding. They also hope that it offers some additional insights into Chinese business practices to aid in some small way the further development of China itself together with further collaboration and mutual understanding between Chinese everywhere and their non-Chinese business associates.

Ying Lun So
Anthony Walker

Acknowledgements

We cannot imagine that any book of this nature can be written without the informal assistance of many colleagues and friends who engage with us in the academic world. Certainly we owe a debt of gratitude to all those who have discussed our ideas with us. But we would especially wish to thank Professor Lawrence Lai and Professor Chau Kwong Wing, both of the University of Hong Kong, for sharing their many insights and understanding over many years.

Y.L. So offers his particular gratitude to Mr William Wong, his intellectual companion since his school days with whom he is sure some of the ideas underpinning this book were formed during the many discussions they have had about Chinese history and culture through the years. Y.L. So also owes an intellectual debt to Professor Steven N.S. Cheung, Professor Emeritus, University of Hong Kong, for bringing the transaction cost paradigm to Hong Kong over 20 years ago just when he had started teaching economics, as well as his crystal clear thinking about the many basic concepts in economics. Professor Cheung made him realize the immense power as well as the great fun of the subject. Also to Professor Douglass North, for his courage in tackling very broad complex subjects, even whole historical trends and cultures. His writings have inspired many ideas in this book.

It seems that many authors thank their wives. We know why and we are no exception. Without our wives' fortitude and unstinting support, this book would simply not have been written. For their understanding we thank them.

Notwithstanding the help and support we have received, we are solely responsible for any faults.

Permission to include material from the following sources was generously given:

http://www.wsu.edu:8001/vcwsu/commons/topics/culture/culture-index.html Accessed June 2004. Permission granted by Dr Richard Law, Washington State University.

Permission to reprint Alchian, Armen A., 'Property Rights', *The Concise Encyclopedia of Economics*, Liberty Fund, Inc., ed. David R. Henderson. Library of Economics and Liberty. http://www.econlib.org/library/Enc/PropertyRights.html granted by David R. Henderson, copyright owner. Accessed May 2004.

An extract from the address 'Convergence and the Judicial Role: Recent Developments in China' by The Hon. J.J. Spigelman AC Chief Justice of New South Wales to the China Education Centre, University of Sydney, 11 July 2002.

1 What is *guanxi*?

Guanxi introduced

Guanxi can be roughly translated as personal ties but the simplicity of the phrase does little justice to the set of meanings and nuances invoked by the word. It has often been seen as a mysterious, yet vital, ingredient in successful Chinese business activities wherever they are carried out. There may be variations in its emphasis among Chinese in different parts of the world but, once understood, its distinctive nature compared to the way business is done among non-Chinese becomes clear.

The significance of *guanxi* is felt not only by businessmen but has also been recognized more formally by academics. Capitalism in Taiwan has been called '*guanxi* capitalism' (Hamilton, 1989). A survey in the Peoples' Republic of China (PRC) found that over 42 per cent of respondents regarded *guanxi* as very important in socio-economic life, while nearly 50 per cent regarded it as either important or somewhat important (Chu and Ju, 1990). It has also been found that the more successful Chinese businessmen in a city in the Philippines used more social connections in their business than did the less successful ones (Omohundro, 1983). No overseas businessman working in the PRC or the other major Chinese business communities of Hong Kong and Taiwan can fail to become familiar with the term *guanxi* but few will understand it. Whilst it will seem intangible, there is no doubt that it has contributed significantly to the success of Chinese entrepreneurs and the places where they work.

Whilst there is wide recognition of the importance of *guanxi* among both businessmen and academics, no explanation has been put forward of why *guanxi* was initiated and developed, what function it serves, how it is maintained and why it is a phenomenon peculiar to Chinese businessmen. An explanation and understanding of *guanxi* is necessary, not only as an aid to overseas (and Chinese) businessmen operating in Chinese business communities, but also for its impact on the wider economic field.

There has been much talk about Asian values in recent years. Before the Asian financial crisis in 1997, Asian values had been cited by some, especially politicians, as being responsible for the 'economic miracles' enjoyed by the dragon and tiger economies of Asia Pacific. Since the Asian financial crisis, Asian values have been blamed for contributing to the crisis. No matter whether one agrees with either of these views, there is no doubt that increasing attention has been paid to the role of cultural values in economic success. The importance placed on personal ties constitutes one of the most important building blocks of the so-called Asian values.

An important issue arising from these views is to what extent the developing Asian economies should imitate the developed economies in the West. The mystique inherent in the word *guanxi* can conjure a commonplace but invalid assumption that the use of personal ties in business is a uniquely Chinese or Asian phenomenon, particularly amongst business visitors to Asia. But, of course, there is a similar emphasis on personal ties in other cultures. In the well-developed market economies of the West, personal ties play a powerful role. Every business relies to a greater or lesser extent on relationships and contacts to ease the business process. However, *guanxi* functions in uniquely Chinese ways and is entrenched and orchestrated to a degree not remotely approached by business relationship systems in other cultures. The significant distinguishing feature of *guanxi* is that fundamentally it is a method of economic organization without resorting to law or other formal rules. Business relationships in other cultures do not have the force of such a basis to sustain them. Before trying to explain and understand *guanxi* more fully, a review of what is currently known is needed. Whilst *guanxi* has become the word that epitomizes the trading style of the Chinese, what exactly is it? A good first insight is given by Edith Terry (1984):

> China is a world where what counts is not only whom one knows, but also who owes whom a favour.

Business relationships

China and the West compared

Business relationships in Western economies oil the wheels of business; they are not a method of economic organization or a substitute for commercial law. In Chinese society *guanxi* serves all these purposes.

In the West business relationships are based on a business culture and can be personal or purely pragmatic (utilitarian). Other relationships e.g. social, family, have their own culture.

But *guanxi* is the totality of any relationship; it is indivisible, pragmatic, or personal and pragmatic, but essentially utilitarian.

The simple translation of the Chinese word *guanxi* is 'relationship'. The same word can be used either to refer to people, when the word means human relationship, or non-human issues, e.g. *guanxi* between price and quantity demanded. However, when the word appears in English and spelt as *guanxi* based on Peking's pin-yin system,[1] it refers only to relationships between people.

Guanxi can be characterized as being personal, as representing the totality of a relationship between two business partners and as being mainly utilitarian in nature. An examination of the many descriptions of *guanxi* illustrates how writers have struggled to put into words the nature of the personal relationships represented by *guanxi*. For example: 'Chinese particularistic ties' (Jacobs, 1982), 'personal ties' (Pye, 1992) and as 'necessitating very personal interactions' (Leung *et al.*, 1993).

However, a one line definition for *guanxi* is misleading because the very reason the Chinese word *guanxi* is used in English text, instead of saying 'particularistic ties', is because a simple English translation is insufficient to bring out the special nature of *guanxi*. Scholars have worked hard at giving texture to its meaning. Examples are:

> It seems to me that either 'particularistic ties' or 'personal network' does carry the meaning of *kuan-his* [*guanxi*], but neither fully grasps the complicated and rich meaning of the word.
>
> (King, 1991)

> And after studying human relationships in the Chinese village of Fengjia, Kipnis (1997) noted that 'the production of *guanxi* simultaneously creates human feeling and material obligation . . . In *guanxi*, feeling and instrumentality are a totality.'

A top Chinese executive in one of Hong Kong's largest companies said one of the primary differences in the Chinese and Western ways of doing business could be traced to the fact that in the West business developed its own culture separate from private or personal culture, with a different set of rules and a character of its own. In the Chinese context there is no separate morality for business. There are no separate rules that divide the conduct of business from that of personal affairs, in which the key factor is proper human relations. A successful business relationship between Chinese companies begins with the establishment of a personal bond between the principal managers of the companies and is based thereafter on the careful maintenance of these personal ties (De Mente, 1992).

It seems that the Chinese are not used to compartmentalizing the different roles that they have with others and so treat the other person according to the requirement of the current role. For example, it is difficult for them to say that 'being my teacher, I should be respectful to you, but now that you are my customer, I have to stick to the normal terms of trade'. This characteristic is indirectly confirmed by the fact that 'some businessmen in the olden times were inclined to leave their hometowns to do business far away. This was to ensure that business could be conducted according to market principles, freeing the parties from interference by the particularistic pressures of *guanxi*' (Skinner, 1971).

An inability to separate different roles has also led to the common saying of *junzhi zi jiao dan ru shui* (friendship between gentlemen is as plain as water). That is, in order to avoid the mutual obligations involved in *guanxi*, gentlemen would rather not develop any close *guanxi* because it is not possible to behave in very different ways when acting in different roles in relation to the same person.

Guanxi therefore has the characteristic of being personalistic or particularistic. It is a connection between people, not firms. Even if an individual is running a number of separate companies, the counter-party considers himself as still trading with the same entity, the person with whom he has *guanxi*. He could not have different relationships with each company.

As *guanxi* is personal in nature; it easily gives the impression that the bond is mainly emotional and affective. However, while affection might be present, because *guanxi* lumps together the different roles that one has with another, it seems that *guanxi* is primarily utilitarian in nature. For example, Walder (1986) characterized *guanxi* as 'instrumental-personal ties'. A Chinese businessman has been quoted as saying 'I know that when I retire – no more parties. You know, people are very pragmatic . . . Hong Kong's memory is short' (Redding, 1990).

Redding went on to highlight the utilitarian nature of *guanxi* as an 'instrumental view of relationships, the opportunistic "using" of other people, [which] is likely to lead to friction only when one of the partners is naïve, and the naïve does not survive in this environment'. That is, if you cannot do anything for me, I will not do anything for you. Such an instrumentalist view of *guanxi* is echoed by other writers, including Yang (1994). For example, when comparing different types of relationship in China, she noted that *guanxi* was high on the 'gain-and-loss' calculation and low on emotional affect.

There are, however, some studies which claim that the closeness of the *guanxi* depends on *ganqing* (loosely translated as emotional affect). If this is the case, then it will contradict the characterization of *guanxi* as utilitarian. For example, Silin (1972) noted:

> When trading relationships exist between two people not linked by traditionally sanctioned solidarities, the individuals concerned simply claim to share *kan-ch'ing* [*ganqing*] or rapport . . . Bonds of *kan-ch'ing* [*ganqing*] invest any association with flexibility and confidence . . . People rarely speak of having confidence in each other; instead they stress the degree of intimacy and warmth between them, the sate of their *kan-ch'ing* [*ganqing*].

Jacobs (1982) also used the term *ganqing* to denote the closeness of *guanxi*. But is it really emotional affection that those interviewed by Silin or Jacobs were referring to when they talked about *ganqing* as the bond between business partners? One interviewee was quoted as saying. 'Of course one can use *ganqing*. If *ganqing* can't be used, it isn't *ganqing*!' (Jacobs, 1982). What is clear is that for this interviewee *ganqing* was rather utilitarian. In fact, those conducting business negotiations often use words hinting at the affective aspects of the relationship. However, those using such words may not genuinely mean what they say. In fact, very often, when deep and genuine feeling exists between the two parties, there will be less explicit reference to the affective aspects of the relationship and bargaining will not be, or at least not explicitly, conducted.

Hence, *guanxi* represents the totality of the relationship between two persons. It is impossible to differentiate the affective aspect of friendship between two individuals and the utilitarian aspects of the business relationship. When one aspect ends, so will the other.

Business relations in the West

In Chinese societies personal relations dominate and are not usually separated from business relationships. Business relations in the West are more technical and company orientated with early recognition of the possible need for contractual formality as illustrated by this extract:

> In business markets, relationships form the backbone of key supplier agreements for larger companies. Where a big company requires a regular delivery of parts or goods for its production processes, it does not just look at the quality of goods or materials to be bought. In these key supplier deals, elements such as delivery flexibility, lead time and technical support are essential to the smooth flow of products through the production cycle. In addition there are normally technology tie-ins the form of machinery, computer software and systems and shared intellectual property (both formal and informal shared knowledge that comes from working together over time).

> The importance of quality of supply and long-term commitment means that purchasers are looking to build strong business relationships with core suppliers. At a contractual level this may mean signing up to Service Level Agreements specifying commitments and penalties or bonuses for achieving certain standards of service. However the SLA is normally a last resort, relationships are worked out in negotiation primarily between the accounts manager and purchaser.

(Compiled from: http://www://dobney.com/Knowledge/customer_relationships_b2b.htm (accessed April 2004))

Initiating, developing and maintaining *guanxi*

Developing and maintaining *guanxi* is essential to its effectiveness. Those not in the know would like to understand how this works but businessmen are reluctant to disclose its intricacies and details. However, some studies have attempted to tie down, albeit in rather general terms, how *guanxi* is initiated, developed and maintained.

Two conditions have often been identified as a necessary precursor to the initiation and development of *guanxi*. The first is the prior existence of a *guanxi* base founded on some commonality between the two persons or, if a *guanxi* base does not exist, then *guanxi* can be initiated through an intermediary who has *guanxi* with both parties. The second is that for the further development and maintenance of *guanxi*, conformity to *renqing* rules, in particular, reciprocity and continued social interaction as well as the utilization of the *guanxi* relationship are essential.

Jacobs (1982) in his study of *guanxi* in Mazu, a town in Taiwan, coined the term '*guanxi* base', which he considered as the starting point for determining the closeness of a *guanxi*:

> [A base of *guanxi* depends on] two or more persons having a commonality of shared identification. That is, each of the persons having a *guanxi* base shares an aspect of personal identification that is important to them as individuals, such as identification with family, hometown, school or place of work. Such identification may be ascribed, e.g., native place or lineage, or it may involve shared experience . . . The Chinese terminology for many *guanxi* explicitly recognizes this commonality: the word *tong* meaning 'same', or 'shared,' is followed by a word describing the commonality such as native-place [*tong-xiang*], education [*tong-shue*] or place of work [*tong-shi*].

As mentioned earlier Jacobs' use of affection (*ganqing*) is problematic. However, his depiction of a *guanxi* base as the starting point from which the closeness of a particular relationship will subsequently develop is shared by other scholars of *guanxi*.

Numazaki (1996) has given numerous examples of how enterprise groups in Taiwan have been brought together through *guanxi* ties that started with some of Jacobs' *guanxi* bases. In his examples, *tongxiang* (same home village), *tongzong* (same surname), *tongnian* (same age), employer/employee relationships, family ties, kinship ties (both paternal and maternal kin) have all been found to contribute to the initiation of *guanxi*, which subsequently developed into very close business cooperation.

The longevity of the *guanxi* base is illustrated by Matteo Ricci (Jacobs, 1982) who described the *guanxi* between classmates that he observed almost four hundred years ago:

> In this acquiring of degrees there really is something worthy of admiration in the relationship that grows up between candidates of the same year. Those whom fortune has brought together in attaining a higher degree look upon one another as brothers for the rest of their lives. There is mutual agreement and sympathy among them, and they help each other and one another's relatives as well, in every possible way.

The Chinese are ingenious in thinking up commonalities! A joke that appeared in the Chinese press about how the Chinese try to make connections even when there is in fact little connection to be found, as quoted by Chiao (1982), is abridged and translated as follows:

> 'My surname is Li,' said Mr. Li.
> 'Oh. My wife's surname is also Li. So I should call you *jiujiu* [uncle on the matrilineal line],' said Chen, shaking the hand of Li vehemently as if he is very lucky in finally meeting with his wife's brother after so many years.
> 'My surname is Cheng,' said another guest.
> 'Oh. So we are one family because I am Chen too!'
> 'No. My name is Cheng, not Chen.'
> 'Oh . . . well, our names sound so close that I would still consider that we're from the same family.'

Non-Chinese may reflect at this point that similar ties also exist in their cultures through similar relationships, and so they do. But as the story unfolds it will become apparent that the strength of the Chinese relationships is more widespread and unquestioning, for compelling reasons, and hence potentially wider and stronger. Whilst a *guanxi* base is extremely important, *guanxi* can still be initiated if a *guanxi* base is weak or non-existent through the use of a *guanxi* reference.

Associations

In the West past associations are of general interest to some people, but no more than that.

School and university reunions are not often arranged. When they are they may be attended but not as a high priority. If they are attended, it is usually out of curiosity rather than for potential business contacts. Also in the West, home towns do not exert a great hold after people have moved on. Attachment has weakened over the last century. In fact many are busy denying their origins!

Contact tends to be kept with a few old friends from the past and acquaintances are drawn from a person's immediate surroundings of their social and work environment. Relationships tend to be kept casual without a sense of mutual dependency.

Not so for the Chinese, associations are carefully and industriously maintained. Reunions are a regular feature of the social scene. Such associations tend to be formalized and ritualized. Strong roots are formed and nurtured building up expectations and obligations in members. And so powerful *guanxi* bases are established from which *guanxi* can be developed.

A *guanxi* reference is an intermediary who has *guanxi* with both parties. A person who wants to develop *guanxi* with someone with whom he does not have *guanxi* will ask the intermediary to introduce them to the person with whom he wants to develop *guanxi*. The importance of the reference person is illustrated by the Chinese saying *bu kan seng mian kan fo mian* (even if you don't give face to the monk, at least you should give face to the Buddha). In this saying the *guanxi* reference is the Buddha and the person with whom *guanxi* is to be developed is the monk.

For example, in response to Yang's (1994) request for an interview for a job, a factory deputy manager said: 'Old Liao and I have been close friends for a long time. Since it was Old Liao who introduced you to me, it must mean he trusts you, so I trust you too. Besides, since you are his friend, helping you is helping him too.'

When Yang noticed that her friend Lin, well versed in *guanxi*, befriended a person who was occupying a not particularly influential position but whose job was rather comfortable she was puzzled.

Lin replied that even though this person may not have direct access to certain opportunities, the fact that he was able to land this job indicates that he probably has access to friends in various influential positions who could be approached through him (Yang, 1994).

Such is the intricacy of *guanxi* development. Whilst parallels can be drawn with relationships in other cultures, the expectation for effective action as a result of *guanxi* is entrenched within Chinese business to a far greater extent. It is not casual or trivial. It is not a hope that perhaps I will be helped in the future; it is practically a guarantee that this will be the case. This is due in no small part to *renqing*.

When developing or maintaining *guanxi* conformity to *renqing* is of vital importance. King (1991) explained that '*Jen-ch'ing [renqing]* is different from *kan-ch'ing [ganqing]*, which is merely sentiment, or an affective component of all human relations. *Kan-ch'ing* is personal, while *jen-ch'ing* is social'. *Renqing* covers not only sentiments but also its social expressions such as the offering of congratulations or condolences or the making of gifts on appropriate occasions (Yang, 1957). *Renqing* has been translated as a person's obligations (Silin, 1972). Ambrose King (1991) wrote that *renqing* could be interpreted as the norms of Chinese interpersonal relationships; rules of propriety, or how to behave.

Many common Chinese expressions illustrate the importance of conforming to *renqing* rules. A person who 'is not well versed in *(bu tong) renqing*' or has no *renqing* flavour (*mei you renqing wei*) is someone who is regarded as being seriously deficient in some vital human skills. If people are accused of acting in a way that is *bu jin renqing* (not close to *renqing*), they are nearly being accused of being inhuman.

A good summary of *renqing* was given by Yan (1996):

> [T]he fundamental principle of interaction and communication at the individual level is encapsulated in *renqing* ethics, which should be understood as first and foremost a set of moral norms that guide and regulate one's behaviour. *Renqing* is also the socially accepted pattern of emotional responses in the sense that one takes others' emotional responses into consideration.

Goodbye, we must lunch sometime

Maintaining contacts in the West is generally a casual affair. Lunch now and then, unless cancelled because something else has cropped up, a drink after work if time can be found. Such activities carry a low priority and often the suggested invitation is not serious or not taken seriously.

Not so for the Chinese. The way one is expected to behave in developing and maintaining *guanxi* (*renqing*) is a stylized way of conducting a relationship in which the moves are clearly understood by both parties. Reciprocity of attention is absolutely necessary if *guanxi* is to be established and preserved. It is much more than good manners and more akin to a courtship dance.

Maintaining *guanxi* requires the expenditure of time and money at an intensity which Westerners can have difficulty accepting and, if accepted, have great difficulty sustaining. The orchestration and elaboration of *guanxi*-moves can irritate Westerners and highlights the clash of cultures.

To act according to *renqing* rules is to put on a human face, but behind this face lurks the demand for reciprocity. One consequence is that gift or banquet-giving both involve much etiquette and polite rituals, which serve to mask or mute the instrumental nature of the gift and to save face for both sides. . . . Such occasions as the Chinese New Year, the birth of a child, weddings and so on provide good opportunities to lay the groundwork (Yang, 1994). An interesting way of looking at banqueting activities in China in terms of the creation of obligations is that 'in a sense, the lifting of every glass of Maotai liquor is a signal that for every *guanxi* member there is an obligation to reciprocate' (Brunner *et al.*, (1989)).

With reciprocity in mind, and as quoted earlier:

> China is a world where what counts is not only whom one knows, but also who owes whom a favour.
>
> (Terry, 1984)

The very common Chinese saying *shouren enhui qiannian ji* (if you receive a favour from another person, you should remember it for at least a thousand years) depicts clearly the strength of the obligation for reciprocity within the rules of *renqing*. There is also the common expression that *renqing jin guo zai* (*Renqing* [debt] should be more urgently repaid than monetary debt). The use of the phrase *zuo renqing* means giving a monetary gift to the host when invited to a banquet for celebrating important events such as a marriage or a person's birthday. This clearly shows the explicit meaning and use of the word *renqing* in the Chinese language. There is nothing subtle about it.

Some Westerners are visibly irritated by this Chinese norm:

> [T]he Chinese are usually single-mindedly trying to build up a relationship in which they will seek to obligate and to shame the Americans into providing special, indeed exceptional, considerations for the Chinese . . . They . . . know what *guanxi* is. Yet, strangely, the Japanese response seems to be one of pulling back and resisting any overtures for the ties of *guanxi* by seeking to be more businesslike and impersonal than most

> American negotiators . . . [T]he Japanese are much more
> sensitive to the potential dangers of backlash by a people whose
> wishes for dependency cannot be gratified.
>
> (Pye, 1992)

However, Chinese behaviour determines that one should have a
clear idea of the extent of the relationship, not acting too intimately,
nor keeping oneself too aloof. In a way, a clear idea of the accounts
of this who-owes-whom game of reciprocity should be maintained
(though only in one's mind) and should not be overused. As
Brunner *et al.* (1989) confirm:

> In the maintenance of a *guanxi*, it is important that each party
> does not overuse *guanxi* to the extent that it becomes a burden
> for the other member. Moreover, one must also remember his
> obligations to the *guanxi* and respond when called upon to give
> his assistance.

To continue to maintain an unbalanced account is a way of
maintaining a relationship. To say that 'from now on, *wuomen
butuo buchien*' (from now on, we owe each other nothing) means
that the relationship is ended and *guanxi* exists no more. But with
the *renqing* advice of *ni jingwo ice, wo jingni ijang* (since you have
paid one foot of respect to me, I shall pay a respect of ten feet to
you in return) mutual indebtedness can only continue to increase
forever!

King (1987) described four possible responses when presented with
a gift:

> To refuse to accept the gift.
> To return the favour immediately and in the same value.
> To return the favour at an appropriate time at a later date.
> To accept the favour but do not return the favour at all.

Only the third is accepted as the normal response and indicates an
intention to maintain a long-term relationship. The first and second
convey the message that there is no intention of maintaining the

relationship at all while the fourth will condemn the recipient as forever a debtor in *renqing* that will result in an unequal relationship.

Guanxi has to start slowly as reflected by one of De Mente's (1992) interviewees: 'We prefer to give the relationship time to develop, to create friendship and trust, and only after we feel secure in the relationship do we go for big deals . . .'

It then has to be continuously maintained otherwise it will wane. Maintenance of *guanxi* is costly and choices have to be made as illustrated by Brunner *et al.* (1989):

> A *guanxi* may diminish in closeness with the passage of time as the need for the closeness ceases to exist, and the time and energy to maintain it cannot be justified . . . [F]requent interaction is essential or its closeness may wither and decline. This emphasis upon social interaction necessitates pressures on the financial capacities and time of the persons required to maintain close *guanxi*. Of these, time is the most crucial. Obviously, one cannot have an unlimited number of *guanxi* established with many persons and be able to develop each of them to the degree expected.

What does *guanxi* provide?

Most studies of *guanxi* or Chinese business networks have, either explicitly or implicitly, established that such connections are extremely important in business affairs.[2]

If there is *guanxi* between two businessmen, each seems willing to grant more favourable terms to the other in business affairs so that deals are more easily struck between them; that is, favours seem to flow when *guanxi* is present. On the face of it deals are struck which appear less profitable to one or both parties than other options which appear readily available but which involve other parties. What is the magic behind *guanxi* that allows this?

It could be because there is an emotional tie between the two businessmen or it may just be a rational business decision. If it is purely because of affection, then the favourable terms are in fact a kind of payment for consumption. As argued earlier, it seems that affection is unlikely to be the reason behind most *guanxi* relationships. Even if affection can account for some *guanxi* behaviour, what is more interesting and puzzling is that the majority of *guanxi* relationships are seen to be rational business practice by the parties involved, even though the agreements entered into do not appear to be so by others not familiar with *guanxi*. It is this aspect of *guanxi* that is most fascinating to outsiders and which this book will seek to explain.

The all-inclusive concept for trade and business cooperation is the transaction, to use an economic term, or deal, to use a business term. The benefits of having *guanxi* can be subsumed under the more general idea that *guanxi* facilitates transactions (or deals). In other words, it is easier to agree on a mutually acceptable price and terms when *guanxi* is present. For the possibility of a deal to take place there must exist some prices which are higher than the lowest acceptable price for the seller and lower than the highest acceptable price for the buyer (that is, there is a net gain in the exchange). Very often however the reason why a deal that is apparently possible between two persons cannot proceed is because the transaction cost involved in such a deal is higher than the total gain for both parties from the deal. So the obvious starting point to look for the magic of *guanxi* in facilitating exchange is the way it lowers the transaction cost (the cost of doing the deal).

Several studies on *guanxi* have explicitly referred to the role of *guanxi* as the reduction of transaction costs, whilst many others implicitly refer to this role by saying that it reduces business risk. So what is the business risk that can be reduced by a close relationship between two trading partners? It must, of course, be a risk that is under the control of either of the two partners, and not risks such as natural disasters or changes in market condition, as these have nothing to do with the relationship between the business partners. The most significant business risk that can be controlled by the partners themselves is the risk of either one of them going back on their word. That is the risk of a default on agreements previously made or of a problem arising from contract enforcement.

This characteristic of *guanxi* is indirectly confirmed by what most *guanxi* studies have given as the magic behind *guanxi* – trust.

Trust

Transaction cost economists, as represented by Williamson (1990), consider trust to be unsound as a contractual safeguard. However, Williamson does not dismiss trust, but distinguishes between personal and commercial trust. He argues that commercial trust has a cost – a transaction cost. The cost of trust is the cost of the risk of trusting your business partner without credible commitments to protect against the performance expected of your business partner not being achieved. In the absence of trust or something similar to *guanxi* in the West, deals have to be secured through formal contractual arrangements that can be enforced through law if necessary. Such protection against opportunism by a business partner can incur high transaction costs. Due to the Western orientation to such arrangements, the reduction in transaction costs achievable through a formalized system of trust such as provided by *guanxi* is not recognized. The argument of Western transaction cost economists relating to trust (that trust has a transaction cost) is sustained by the characteristics of *guanxi* but in a form not recognized by them.

For example, Dannhaeuser (1981) in his study of Chinese business methods in the Philippines observed the construction of networks of trust of vertically integrated companies which controlled a total market process, but they did so by informal processes only. These networks served to reduce uncertainty and transaction costs, for instance over the risk of credit. Also Redding (1997) noted:

> Trust is a rare commodity and that is part of its value. Much of the daily behaviour of the Chinese businessman lies in building and maintaining his personal network of trusted others.

Trust

Some contrasting Western quotations on trust show the West's ambivalence:

'Trust everybody, but cut the cards.'
(Finley Peter Dunne)

'It is an equal failing to trust everybody, and to trust nobody.'
(English Proverb)

'A man who doesn't trust himself can never really trust anyone else.'
(Cardinal De Retz)

'Love all, trust a few, do wrong to none.'
(William Shakespeare)

'One must be fond of people and trust them if one is not to make a mess of life.'
(E.M. Forster)

'I think we may safely trust a good deal more than we do.'
(Henry David Thoreau)

'You may be deceived if you trust too much, but you will live in torment unless you trust enough.'
(Frank Crane)

'In God we trust, all others we virus scan.'
(Author unknown)

(Compiled from: www.quotegarden.com/trust.html www.annabelle. net/topics/trust.php (accessed April 2004))

As we have seen earlier on *renqing* and the creation of obligations, *guanxi* is often initiated and maintained by the offering of a favour by one party to the other. The other party then feels obligated to return the favour some day. Apart from the *renqing* rule behind the signal of goodwill on the part of the provider of the favour and the tacit creation of a contract-like obligation on the part of the receiver, it also requires the provider of a favour to trust that the other party not only feels obligated but will actually carry out his part of the deal in the future in returning the favour.

But it seems that trust is at best a starting point for understanding *guanxi*. Certainly the depth of trust in many other cultures is not so entrenched or as reliable as in *guanxi* as illustrated by Arrow (in Swedberg, 1990):

> In a rational type of analysis it will be said that it is profitable to be trustworthy. So I will be trustworthy because it is profitable to me. But you can't very easily establish trust on a basis like that. If your basis is rational decision and your underlying motive is self-interest, then you can betray your trust at any point when it is profitable and in your interest to do so. Therefore other people can't trust you.

Trust is a handy explanation but its problem is that it assumes the problem away. Why should one person trust another person? There has to be a basis, a reason for the trust. That is, the person trusts not because he is by nature a trusting person, but because he finds the other person trustworthy even if selfish. In fact, Chinese businessmen are notorious for not being very trusting. For example there is the common saying that *hai ren zhi xin bu ke you; fang ren zhi xin bu ke wu* (a heart for harming others must not be harboured; a heart for defending against others must not be lacking). Chinese businessmen are well aware of opportunistic behaviour[3] and that is probably why they have developed elaborate ways to secure exchange without the sanction of the law. *Guanxi* is basically utilitarian and brings material benefits to both parties. This makes *guanxi* the more puzzling because business rationality should then dictate and trust cannot be attributed to the affective aspects of the relationship. So it is necessary to look further to find an answer to this puzzle.

Partnering

Partnering has emerged in the USA, UK and other Western economies as a form of collaboration between companies working together on construction projects, particularly between clients and contractors but also between contractors and sub-contractors. One of its major aims is to improve cooperation and reduce the adversarial nature of the industry.

The underlying reasons for the development of partnering are to reduce transaction costs below those for other forms of contractual relationship that rely on costly contractual arrangements. It attempts to do so by basing the relationship between the parties on trust as a protection from opportunism, which essentially means 'self-interest seeking'.

Theoretically partnering should not require contractual agreements between the parties but in reality they are invariably used but with the expectation that they will not be relied upon!

Whilst the reliance on trust in partnering in the West could be seen to be akin to a *guanxi* system, the need to back it up with a formal contract with third party enforcement shows that this is not so. When *guanxi* exists formal enforceable contracts are not needed – in Chinese societies either trust or enforceable contracts, in the West both.

Interestingly, partnering has not taken off, or at least not successfully, in Hong Kong and China both of which are strong in *guanxi*.

2 Explaining *guanxi*

Guanxi has often been criticized as a form of nepotism: unfair, inefficient and in general detrimental to business and economic growth, although it may yield benefits to the individuals who possess *guanxi*. But if it is really that bad, how has it survived? Are judgements being passed too soon? Maybe some understanding about why the phenomenon has occurred is needed to temper critics or even eliminate them.

While descriptions of *guanxi,* or the network structure of business among the Chinese, are plenty, those purporting to explain or even just to make sense of its existence are relatively scarce. Of the explanations given, the majority is what might be termed cultural explanations. That is, they relate *guanxi* to Chinese culture. Few of them explicitly state that there is a causal relationship between Chinese culture and the predominance of personal relationships in business, but most would agree that *guanxi* should be understood in the context of Chinese culture.

Besides cultural explanations, theorists from the institutional school of organizational studies have also tried to provide an organizational institutionalist explanation. While the culturalists are keener on providing descriptions, not explanations, of Chinese culture and then placing *guanxi* as merely one manifestation of this peculiar culture, the organizational institutionalists are much more enthusiastic about providing a theory to explain the way businesses are organized among the Chinese.

As for economists, attempts to directly attack the issue of *guanxi* or the prominence of personal relationships in business among the Chinese are rare. Landa (1981 and 1983) has tried to explain the network structure among the Chinese as an ethnically homogeneous middleman group. The emphasis was on homogeneity and not Chineseness. Another important attempt was made by Ben-Porath (1980). He did not directly confront the Chinese way of doing business, but his object of explanation – the 'f-connection', family, friends and firm, obviously has great relevance to *guanxi*. Both are attempts at economic explanations and both utilized transaction cost as their guiding paradigm.

What follows are critical reviews of the success of each of the three approaches in explaining *guanxi* which then lead to a choice-theoretic approach based on the maximization postulate in economics, adopted to guide an explanation of *guanxi* as well as to organize contributions from various disciplines.

Interdisciplinary approaches

(Academic) disciplines themselves have been described as stable systemic communities within which researchers concentrate their experience into a particular worldview. This has benefits in terms of the efficiency of communication and interaction within the discipline (including, for example, assessment of quality or the verification of knowledge claims) but puts limits on the kinds of questions they can ask about their material, the methods and concepts they use, the answers they believe and their criteria for truth and validity (Thompson, 1990).

Progress can only be made by recognizing the validity of different types of knowledge and approaches to research problems. Individuals who are confined by their disciplines may only see part of a problem, the part they are trained to recognize, and will use familiar methods to try to solve it. Researchers with contrasting backgrounds working together often develop innovative solutions that can liberate the research process (outcome of a dinner discussion, held in May 2000 by the Royal Geographical Society).

Solutions to the world's problems have always needed an interdisciplinary approach. Only in recent times has this been fully recognized. This applies in equal measure to explaining the historical base of social phenomena such as *guanxi*.

A Chinese culture perspective

Few writers have said explicitly that Chinese tradition and culture is an explanation of why the Chinese handle their social relationships in the way they do or more specifically, why the Chinese everywhere seem to rely so heavily on *guanxi*. But they somehow suggest that a mere description of Chinese culture would somehow enhance our understanding of this phenomenon. This is only natural because it seems that the Chinese, no matter where found, whether in mainland China, Taiwan, Hong Kong, Southeast Asia or in the West, display similarities in terms of how they do business based on or through the building up of personal relationships. They only differ in degree.

As for what Chinese culture stands for, many have taken Chinese culture to mean Confucianism while others, though still taking Confucianism as having the main influence on Chinese culture, have also included other elements such as Taoism and Buddhism.

There is no doubt that Confucianism has had a profound influence in defining Chinese culture. Scholars have characterized Confucianism in terms of the importance it places on relationships in defining the person, on family and kinship ties as the basic building blocks of social order and its behavioural rules based on *ren* and *li*. As a result many have used Confucianism as a proxy for Chinese culture to demonstrate its distinctive characteristics compared to Western philosophies:

. . . most Chinese learning has been the study of human behaviour rather than theoretical knowledge. The pursuit of theoretical knowledge is neither the starting point nor the final goal. The literal translation of Chinese academic thought as philosophy is rather misleading. If we borrow the term it should be qualified as 'philosophy of life'. Chinese philosophy took for its starting point the study of human beings, in which the most important subject was how to behave as a man, how one can truly be called a man, and what kind of relationships exists among men.[1]

Confucianism

K'ung Fu Tzu (Confucius in English) was born in 551 BC in China in what is known now as Shantung Province. He lived during the Chow dynasty, known for its moral laxity. Later in life he wandered through China giving advice to various rulers. He accumulated a band of disciples and during the last years of his life he devoted himself to teaching. His writings deal with individual morality and ethics and the proper exercise of power by the rulers.

Although not having many of the elements of other religions like Christianity and Islam, and not organized as a religion, it has deeply influenced East Asian spiritual and political life in a manner comparable to a religion. It is primarily an ethical system to which important rituals have been added at important times during one's life. Confucian ethical teaching stresses *ren* (humaneness, benevolence), signifying excellent character in accord with *li* (ritual norms), *zhong* (loyalty to one's true nature), *shu* (reciprocity), and *xiao* (filial piety). Together these constitute *de* (virtue).

Mencius, Xunzi and others sustained Confucianism, but it was not influential until Dong Zhongshu emerged in the second century BC. Confucianism was then recognized as the Han state cult and the Five Classics became the core of education. In spite of the influence of Taoism and Buddhism, Confucian ethics have had the strongest influence on the moral fabric of Chinese society.

The Five Classics as we have them today have gone through much editing and alteration by Confucius' disciples, yet there is much in them that can be considered the work of Confucius.

The Five Classics are:

The Book of Changes (I Ching.): The I Ching is a collection of eight triagrams and 64 hexagrams, which consist solely of broken and unbroken lines. These lines were supposed to have great meaning if the key were discovered.

The Book of Annals (Shu King): This is a work of the history of the five preceding dynasties. The example of the ancients was crucial to Confucius' understanding of how the superior man should behave.

The Book of Poetry (Shih Ching): The book of ancient poetry was assembled by Confucius because he believed the reading of poetry would aid in making a man virtuous.

The Book of Ceremonies (Li Chi): This work taught the superior man to act in the right or traditional way. Again Confucius stressed doing things in the same way as the ancients.

The Annals of Spring and Autumn (Chun Chiu): This book, supposedly written by Confucius, gave a commentary on the events of the state of Lu at Confucius' time.

None of these works contain the unique teaching of Confucius but are rather an anthology of works he collected and from which he taught. Confucius' own teachings have come down from four books written by his disciples. They are:

The Analects: This is the most important source we have on Confucius. The Analects are sayings of both Confucius and his disciples.

continued

The Great Learning: This work, which deals with the education and training of a gentleman, comes not from the hand of Confucius but rather from a later period (about 250 BC).

The Doctrine of the Mean: This work deals with the relationship of human nature to the order of the universe. Authorship is uncertain (part of it may be attributed to Confucius' grandson Tzu-Ssu), but it does not come from Confucius.

The Book of Mencius: Mencius wrote the first exposition of Confucian thought about 300 BC by collecting earlier teachings and attempting to put them down systematically. This work, which has had great influence and gives an idealistic view of life, stresses the goodness of human nature.

(Compiled from: www.ishwar.com/confucianism, www.greatcom.org /resources/handbook_of_todays_religions/03chap04/, www.inquiry. net/ideals/faiths/chinese.htm (accessed April 2004))

In terms of the Chinese way of looking at oneself, Redding (1980) noted that in the Chinese perception, the idea of a person includes his relationships and is not analysable separately from them. Mead (1934) noted that unlike Christianity, which puts individuals in reference to God, Confucianism relates individuals to their significant others, such as father and uncle in the family, and teacher and master in one's career development. Bian and Ang (1997) reinforce the point by saying:

> [The] self is identified, recognized, and evaluated in terms of one's relations to the groups and communities to whom one belongs. This lays both the abstract and the concrete foundations for *guanxi* to operate in Chinese societies, both in and outside of China.

These characteristics are reflected in the language by Hsu (1971) who uses a common expression to illustrate the influence of the relationships of the person in Confucian thought:

The Chinese conception of man . . . is based on the individual's transactions with his fellow human beings. When the Chinese say of so and so, 't'a pu shih jen' [tab u shi ren] (he is not jen), they do not mean that this person is not a human animal. Instead, they mean that his behaviour in relation to other human beings is not acceptable . . . But the concept of jen [ren] puts the emphasis on interpersonal transactions . . . [I]t sees the nature of the individual's external behaviour in terms of how it fits or fails to fit the interpersonal standards of society and culture.

The word *guanxi* has not been used in the Confucian classics, but the word *lun* is often used and is given great importance. 'Lun means order or, more specifically, "differentiated order" among individuals' (King, 1991). As pointed out by Pan (1948), the Confucian concept of *lun* is basically concerned with two problems: the kind of differentiation to be made between individuals, and the kind of relations to be established between individuals.

The importance placed on relationships and the elaborate way that Confucians define *lun* can be seen in their description of the *Wulun* (the five cardinal relations): *qing* (affection) between parent and child, *yi* (righteousness) between ruler and subject; *bie* (distinction) between husband and wife; *xu* (order) between brothers; and *xin* (sincerity, trust) between friends (King, 1991).

Yang Lien-sheng (1957) has often been cited as an important proponent of the idea that the cultural value of 'reciprocity' (*bao*) has been important in human relationships from ancient to late imperial times and that Confucian ethics and philosophy was one of the three sources of reciprocity.[2]

The ethic of reciprocity was already established in ancient texts. The Confucian classic, the *Book of Rites* states:

> In the highest antiquity they prized (simply conferring) good; in the time next to this, giving and repaying was the thing attended to. And what the rules of propriety value is that of reciprocity. If I give a gift and nothing comes in return, that is

contrary to propriety; if the thing comes to me, and I give nothing in return, which also is contrary to propriety.[3]

And the Han scholar Liu Hsiang in his *Shuo-yuan* or 'Garden of Sayings' remarked:

> Confucius says, 'Virtue is not left to stand alone. (He who practices it) will have neighbours.' Worthy bestowers of kindness will not expect gratitude, while grateful receivers of grace will certainly make a return . . . Now even birds, beasts, and insects understand the principles of co-operation and reciprocity . . . All sources and roots of disaster and disorder come from failure in returning grace.[4]

Guanxi has also been traced by culturalists to the emphasis on family and kinship ties enshrined in Confucianism. In fact, a whole book called the *Xiaojing* was devoted to filial piety and had become a widely read text on filial obedience when China was still under Dynastic rule. *Er-xi-si xiao* (The Twenty-Four Stories on Filial Piety) is also an extremely popular collection of stories about filial piety. With family and kinship as a dominant element in thought, it manifested itself as a model in various other areas of social life (Baker, 1979). The emperor was sometimes called *junfu* (emperor-father) while his subordinates were called *chenzi* (subordinate-son). Chinese call government officials, who are sent to be governors of some locality, *fumu guan* (father/mother-official) while the ruled are called *zimin* (son-subject). Teachers especially of arts and crafts or martial arts are called *sifu* (teacher-father). Friends are brothers or sisters (if they are similar age) or uncles or aunts (if there is a significant difference in age).

In fact, family ties served as a basic model on which other relationships, and ultimately the social order was built:

> [The Confucian scholars] agreed unanimously that the realization of benevolence must begin with the love of children toward their parents. This means that, in the complicated relations among men, filial piety forms the primary and most

fundamental unit of mutual connection between two or more persons, in which the practice of benevolence must first be fulfilled. By inference, all other relations among human beings should emanate from this basic virtue as their source; otherwise, one may not stay on the right course of benevolence for the attainment of peace and prosperity.

(Hsieh, 1967)

A further elaboration of the strong relationship orientation of Confucianism is contained within the meaning of *ren* and *li*; two crucial virtues within the Confucian system.

The two parts that form the Chinese character for *ren*, when taken separately, mean two human beings. Carmody and Carmody (1983) have given a good explanation of the meaning of *ren*:

> *Ren* is humaneness; what makes us human. We are not fully human simply by receiving life in a human form. Rather, our humanity depends upon community, human reciprocity. *Jen* pointed in that direction. It connected with the Confucian golden rule of not doing to others what you would not want them to do to you. Against individualism, it implied that people have to live together hopefully, even lovingly. People have to cultivate their instinctive benevolence, their instinctive ability to put themselves in another's shoes. That cultivation was the primary educational task of Confucius and Mencius.

Confucians attach an importance to *li* similar to that of *ren*. Confucius once said: '*Bu xue li, woo yi li*' (If you don't learn *li*, then you can never stand up as a full human being.). The reason why *li* is so important is because it is a means to achieve *ren* as illustrated by the often quoted saying by Confucius: '*Ke ji fu li wei ren*'. (To restrain the self and conform to *li* is *ren*.)

But what exactly is *li*? Taken literally, *li* can be translated variously as politeness or good manners. However, the word goes deeper than good manners. 'Gentlemanly conduct' (Redding, 1990) and 'propriety' (Yang, 1994) capture the meaning better. Redding (1990) elaborated on the meaning of *li* as follows:

Less a set of rituals than a cultivating of sensitivity to what is appropriate at any time, it provides the lubrication necessary to reduce friction and it fosters the sublimating of self-indulgence in daily interaction.

There might be equivalence of *li* in the West, but the difference lies in the centrality that the Chinese give to appropriate behaviour. 'It has, for Confucian Chinese, moved to the core of life' (Redding, 1990).

Confucianism and Christianity

Confucianism puts people in reference to their relationships with others. Christianity puts people in relationship to God. Christianity stresses God's love for the world and an individual's love of God. God's message is to love one another. Confucianism's message is similar but has no such intermediary.

These differences and similarities between Confucianism as a humanistic tradition and Christianity as a theocentric religion are contained in their fundamental principles, namely *agape* (Christian love) in Christianity and *jen (ren)* (benevolence) in Confucianism.

> Although both *jen (ren)* and Agape are aiming at human transcendence, *jen (ren)* finds its way to transcendence in being virtuous and Agape in responding to God's call . . . two kinds of human love: *jen (ren)* as an extension of one's virtue to others, and Agape as a manifestation of human response to God's love, by which the universality of human love both in Confucianism and in Christianity shine out.
>
> (Yao, 1996)

On the face of it, the similarities between the messages of Confucianism and Christianity are strong, for example:

Confucius, *The Analects, Book XV, Chapter XXIII*

Tsze-hung asked, 'Is there one word which may serve as a rule of practice for all one's life?' The Master said, 'Is not reciprocity such a word? What you do not want done to yourself, do not to others'.

The Bible

Luke 6.31

And as you would that men should do to you, do you also to them likewise.

Matthew 7.12

Therefore all things whatsoever you would that men should do to you, do you even so to them: for this is the law and the prophets.

But the differences are also marked as illustrated by this Confucian text:

One day, a disciple came and asked Confucius what should Shun (a legendary sage king in ancient China) do if his father commits a murder. Confucius said that he should resign from office and take his father to hide at a distant place so his father won't be caught and punished.

His reasoning is that filial piety is more important than justice. Christians would believe that Jesus' solution to the similar problem would be to take up the punishment in place of the actual murderer, for by doing so he would have fulfilled both love and justice. For Confucians 'sin' (or inappropriate behaviour) is defined solely by the relationship held with the other person and is not as defined by a god.

continued

The nature of Confucianism, with no intermediary, acts directly and only on the relationship of individuals and so forms a powerful base for the development of *guanxi*.

(Compiled from: www.east-west-dialogue.tripod.com/dialogue/id2. html, www.lamp.ac.uk/~yao/book.htm, www.sundayschool teachers. org/lesson-confucianism-and-Christianity.htm (accessed April 2004))

Cultural explanations have been criticized by Yang (1994):

> One problem with [the conclusion that Chinese culture is in essence personalistic, kinship-oriented] is not that it is false or misleading, but that it is simply a truism that fails to situate this aspect of the culture in a dynamic with other changing cultural and social structural features . . . The other problem is that it represents an historical approach to Chinese culture which fails to take into account the historical waxing and waning of personalism and neglects the examination of the changing and variable forms in which personalism is historically constructed and reconstructed.

In other words, a cultural explanation fails because culture itself is changing, and this change in culture cannot be explained by culture itself.

A similar criticism comes from organizational institutionalists. They usually regard such cultural explanations as valuable but criticize them for their inadequacy in accounting for change over time and variations in economic organization of countries under a similar Confucian culture.

This is similar to Wrong's (1961) more general criticism of sociologists who take social factors such as culture as the sole factors in influencing human behaviour in his much quoted article 'The Oversocialized Conception of Man' as it makes human beings cultural robots.

These criticisms, while valid, are not necessarily fatal to cultural explanations. Economists have not responded directly to the cultural explanation of *guanxi*. However, it seems that culture, in general, is not often included as a factor in economists' explanations of real world phenomena. DiMaggio (1994) commented:

> Given the centrality of culture to every other social science discipline, how do we explain the low profile in economics? Partly this is a matter of strategy: Economists favour parsimonious deductive models, usually aimed at high levels of abstraction and generality. By contrast, cultural variables have an inevitable grittiness: they present 'differentiae of an irreducible nature', which lead away from elegant quantitative models toward taxonomic specificity. Faced with anomalies in human decision-making, economists prefer cognitive psychology to cultural anthropology: how much easier to incorporate into one's models decision heuristics that are invariant and hard-wired than to deal with perturbations caused by culturally varying schemes of perception and value.

Another strategy adopted by economists when faced with apparently cultural phenomena is to relegate cultural factors to values and tastes, which are taken as givens and therefore exogenous. This, of course, is an admission of ignorance or, to put it more generously, this is not the job of economists. However, to do this with the problem in hand, is to abandon a large portion of the task of explaining *guanxi*. Kipnis (1997) said that '[p]resenting [*guanxi*] as mere pursuit of economic or political interest masks the cultural and historical background that allows social agents to communicate and to form effectively the social relationships that come to be called *guanxi*'. In fact, if economists really want to investigate human institutions, then consideration of such factors seems essential. One of the few economists who recognizes this problem is the institutional economist Douglass North who tried to incorporate informal constraints (North, 1990) into this model in explaining economic performance over time.

Given the enormous amount of resources devoted to the inculcation of Chinese values and culture, economists would be contradicting themselves in ignoring the importance of culture. They would be saying that such efforts are wasted, a proposition that is inconsistent with the maximization postulate.

However, this does not mean that the cultural explanation should be accepted uncritically as the cultural explanation does suffer from the various problems that its critics have cited. However, the answer to such criticisms is not to abandon a cultural explanation out of hand but rather to improve it.

The cultural explanation is vague in that there is often an ambiguity in the exact relationship between culture and *guanxi*. So the way culture has affected *guanxi* practice needs to be clarified. As the cultural explanation may not be the only factor, other factors that might have accounted for the success of *guanxi* behaviour need identifying by looking into the details of the workings of *guanxi* as identified earlier. Culture, at first sight, does not seem to fit into the deductive models favoured by economists. This should be taken as a challenge to provide such a model. Instead of pretending that culture does not exist or does not matter, what economists should do is incorporate the role of culture into an explanatory framework that is consistent with the maximization postulate of economics.

An organizational institutionalist explanation

An alternative to the cultural explanation of the network structure of business in East Asia is offered by organization institutionalists as part of the general surge in institutional theories among sociologists in the late 1970s and 1980s. They have worked on Asian business practices and network structures in Taiwan, Japan and Korea in particular but have yet to formalize their approach. This is probably because the approach of the organizational institutionalists in general has not yet matured, which is reflected in their theory of Asian organizations.

Institutional theory

Organizational institutionalists use institutional theory to study the role of institutions in society. Institutions have been defined as: 'the rules of the game in a society, or more formally, are the humanly devised constraints that shape human interaction. Institutions reduce uncertainty by providing a structure to everyday life' (North, 1990). This is just one of the many definitions given in the literature. There are many different approaches to institutional theory. Each discipline seems to have its own approach.

Institutions are formed through a process of institutionalization through things such as the conventions and rules of conduct that human beings devise to shape human interaction or as an outcome of the 'habituation of action' (Zucker, 1983) in which day-to-day activities become sedimented (survival of structures across generations of organizational members).

Despite the proliferation of literature there is little consensus with regard to 'the measures and methods' associated with institutional theory (Tolbert and Zucker, 1996). Few have examined the mechanisms by which social activities are rendered routine: 'institutionalization is a core process in the creation and perpetuation of enduring social groups' (Berger and Luckman, 1966).

Whilst the study of social groups in general is at the heart of institutional theory, much of the work of organizational institutionalists has focused on more formal organizations. Institutionalist approaches to organizations emphasize that organization structures emerge in particular social contexts. The analyst must understand the institutional preconditions for particular types of organizational structure and design. Two broad approaches are distinguishable. Business systems theories emphasize the need to examine how national social institutions (the nature of the family, religion, culture, education, financial institutions, the state) create a framework of rules and resources which management draw on,

continued

reinforce and change when they structure and design organizations. Neo-institutionalist theories examine how and why ideas about the nature of organizations emerge and are spread from one sector or sphere to another.

(Compiled from: http://www.utwente.nl/cheps/documenten/susu 2003/lub.pdf, http://www.londondegree.org/Organisation_Theory. htm, http://www.business.mmu.ac.uk/research/wps/papers/wp01_ 16.pdf (accessed May 2004))

Nevertheless, theirs is, to date, the most sophisticated theory on Chinese business networks outside economics. They pose questions for anyone who attempts to explain *guanxi* from an economics perspective and their concepts are a constructive source for how a theory of *guanxi* might be formulated.

The institutionalist approach to Asian organization grew out of a reaction to cultural and economic explanations. They appreciated the value of cultural and market explanations but thought them inadequate and offered their own theory to integrate them. Their criticisms of cultural explanations have been discussed earlier.

As for economic explanations, institutionalists have, on the whole, only responded to Alfred Chandler (1977), whom they regard as relying solely on economic causes. Basically, Alfred Chandler's theory rests on technological causes.[5] He did not explicitly incorporate institutions or transaction costs into his theory. Of the transaction cost school, institutionalists have only addressed and in a very brief manner, Oliver Williamson's perspective, claiming that his central concepts are 'difficult to operationalize' (Biggart, 1997). Contributions of other institutionalists and the transaction cost school within economics have been ignored.

Organizational institutionalists are dissatisfied with Chandler's theory because, when applied to organizational forms in Asia, it yielded 'ambiguous results' (Biggart *et al.*, 1992). With the enormous growth in markets in Asia, the sort of large hierarchical structures of Chandler's modern business enterprises have not emerged to the extent predicted. The network structures (informal as well as formal) that are so popular in Asia are not explained by Chandler. Organizational institutionalists reason why Chandler's theory enjoyed relative success explaining the evolution of organizational forms in the West while meeting with relative failure when applied to Asian economies is that the assumptions adopted by Chandler, including 'the idea that economic actors are rational and autonomous, and that they seek self-interest independent of social relations or characteristics' (Biggart *et al.*, 1997) corresponds better to the beliefs in individual autonomy and economic rationality that are behind Western institutions. His theory is able to capture the institutional characteristics of American and European societies but such assumptions fit Asian economies poorly as they do not have the same institutional heritage. Thus it seems that Chandler's theory (what Biggart *et al.* regard as the neoclassical paradigm) is too parochial. It might be inferred that the neoclassical paradigm in economics can only be applied to the particular economies in the West where rationality and autonomy are accepted as universal truths by their societies. That is why organizational institutionalists have attached 'Western bias' in many attempts to explain Asian organizations. This leads them to the idea that:

> Persuasive explanations for the success of Asian business will ultimately come from an institutional analysis of Asian societies and the economies that are embedded in them. Explanations will not come – indeed, cannot come – from attempts to apply a theory rooted in western experience to an alien institutional arena.
>
> (Biggart *et al.*, 1997)

Or put more succinctly: what makes China, China, cannot be learnt from a theory about Europe (Hamilton, 1985).

Institutionalists' efforts to explain Asian business practices throw up interesting contrasts of institutionalists' and economists' methods. First, organizational institutionalists' claim that each country should have its own theory to explain its peculiar characteristic organizational form is problematic. It is commonly held by economists that an explanation is in fact inadequate as an explanation if it is based on a theory that cannot claim any level of generality beyond the question in hand. They believe that institutionalists' way of looking at theory is in great danger of offering *ad hoc* explanations.

Second, it seems that organizational institutionalists have misunderstood the role of the maximization and rationality postulate in economics. Because they found that the particular values and institutions of Asia do not seem to conform to the economic postulate that people are individualist, rational, and selfish, they claimed that Asia's behaviour is at odds with what is predicted by such theories. But what they fail to realize is that even people in the West do not conform to this postulate either! However, this does not mean that a theory will necessarily fail to serve its purpose of explanation and prediction.

The test of the realism of the assumptions of a theory does not amount to a test of the theory itself. Economic theory never says that individuals really think rationally in their daily endeavours. In fact, it would be extremely irrational to be always calculative because our mental resources are scarce and have to be allocated to endless tasks that require such resources. What the postulate says is just that people behave as if they are rational maximizing individuals, just as birds fly in a way as if they know the theories of aerodynamics.

If fact, as will be elaborated later, the rationality or the maximization postulate is adopted as a matter of methodology by economists and is not intended as an accurate description of what is actually going on in people's minds.

It is ironical that many organizational institutionalists praise the peculiar institutional arrangements that have evolved in various Asian economies claiming that such institutions fit local conditions (see for example Hamilton, 1985) and are therefore the most suitable form. Now this in fact affirms, rather than rejects, the choice-theoretic approach of the economist who says that human beings are rational and that benefits are maximized under such arrangements. For what is efficiency if it does not mean a response that fits the situation? It further affirms economists' understanding of the assumption of rationality, that they need not be realistic (in the sense of people being actually calculative and selfish).

The institutional school of organizational analysis does not have a unified theoretical approach (Scott, 1987). However, institutionalists' various approaches share several common features. They:

> ... reject explanations for organizational structure and functioning that rest solely on technical issues such as task requirements, size, and market factors. Moreover, institutionalists tend to view organizations as socially constructed – a product of actors' subjective realities – rather than as objective, material artefacts. Institutionalists do not deny the material impulse behind organizing, such as orientation towards profit, but seek further than economic rationality for explanations of the structures people manufacture in their pursuit of gain.
>
> (Biggart, 1997)

Guanxi networks as explained by organizational institutionalists would then take the form of Chinese organizations as informed by distinctly Chinese organizational logic; one of the most important being patrilineal logic. Institutionalists regard the understanding of such principles as crucial, as they 'inform predictable social relations in multiple arenas, including the economic, and are supported in various ways by state agencies' (Orru, *et al.*,1997).

From culture, institutions are built which then become a more proximate cause of behaviour. The institutions are not independent of culture but they are more concrete manifestations. Based on theories of the social construction of reality, Biggart argues that such institutions acquire a life of their own and reproduce themselves as members uncritically take such institutions as real and universal and as how things have always been done. Internalizing the logic behind such institutions, they proceed to reproduce them, leading to the persistence of such institutions.

Although institutionalists do not take such institutions as the sole explanation of business organizations, this nonetheless is the most distinct feature of their approach. However, though there is some

truth in the way the internalization, externalization and reproduction of institutional logic has contributed to the persistence of
certain business practice, such persistence is by no means eternal.

So where does the organizational logic of the Chinese and their
accompanying social institutions come from and how does it
change? Hamilton regards historical development as the key to
social change:

> [O]rganizational structure is situationally determined, and
> therefore the most appropriate form of analysis is one that taps
> the historical dimension.
>
> (Hamilton *et al.*, 1997)

This is a rather odd explanation because history is just data. It is
itself an object of explanation. On the specific issue of *guanxi*, no
institutionalists have explored in-depth the historical development
that has led to its prominence.

Because of the continuity of time, every present moment must lead
from a prior moment. So in this chronological sense, everything that
happens at the prior moment 'causes' everything that happens at
this moment. Such an explanation is rather devoid of meaning
exactly because it is nearly always true. It might be claimed that the
organizational institutionalists do have the merit of directing us to
examine what has happened a moment ago to understand what is
happening now. But of all the myriad things that were happening
a moment ago, which should we look at? If what is meant is that
we should just examine the significant events, only those that can
be properly classified as historic, then let us not forget that history
is always interpreted and that whether an event or a factor is
significant or not always depends on the theories and concepts with
which we abstract what is significant.

Despite the various problems of the organizational institutionalists'
approach, nonetheless they provide several valuable insights. They
also raise several important issues that any rational choice-theoretic
theory of *guanxi* must address.

The choice-theoretic approach

Explaining human behaviour in terms of the choices and actions of individuals is, or should be, the primary business of economics.

The basis of the choice-theoretic approach that underlies micro-economics is the fundamental assumption of scarcity and hence competition.

The essential element of the choice-theoretic framework of economics is the idea of the rational individual who seeks to maximize utility.

First, their account of the reproduction of organizational logic can account for the persistence of institutions and the survival of long time social or business practices that might seem to have become out of date. Through the insights of 'social constructionist' arguments, they have advanced the cultural argument by tying culture down to an ideology and then elaborating on how such ideology dominates people's behaviour and thus explains its power. However, if we are to use a choice-theoretic approach to *guanxi*, then the apparent inefficiency involved in such persistence has to be reconciled. Furthermore, if there is persistence in cultural ideology, then we have to offer a satisfactory mechanism by which such ideology will change – something that organizational institutionalists have failed to address.

Although there is a serious problem in the resort to history to account for social change, the main problem lies not in the resort to history *per se*, but to the way it is done. If we recognize persistence in cultural ideology, then to tap the historical dimension is natural. However, the way that this should be done is to go back to history to explore why one pattern and not another has evolved. In other words, after citing history, one should then go on to explain it.

Also, by criticizing Alfred Chandler's economic explanation, institutionalists have also prompted anyone who attempts a choice-theoretic approach to reconcile the apparent contradiction between its assumptions and the apparent fact that people are less calculating and concerned more about non-economic goals than economic goals. Institutionalists have pointed out that people do not live in a void. They have cultural backgrounds and they live in a web of social institutions that constrain their behaviour. This is a fact that economists and the choice-theoretic approach cannot deny. How a choice-theoretic approach can be reconciled with the apparent situation where the individual really does not have much choice to make regarding their cultural backgrounds requires explanation.

Economic explanations

Not much has been written on *guanxi* from an economics perspective. More has been written on corruption in PRC business but this is not *guanxi*. Here a line is drawn between *guanxi* and corruption because, though related, they are due to different reasons.

Only two studies related in some way to *guanxi*, arise from economics. They are studies by Ben-Porath (1980) and Landa (1981 and 1983).

Ben-Porath used a transaction cost approach to explain the significance of the family in the organization of exchange (or 'trade' if a business term is used, although 'trade' has a more narrow meaning). He did not address the use of personal ties in any particular country, culture or economic setting. It was intended as a generic analysis of family as an organization of exchange. Though his work is not directly about *guanxi*, it nonetheless provides several insights that are useful in an economic analysis of *guanxi*.

The transaction cost approach

The transaction cost approach emerged from the seminal work of the economist Coase (1937) in which he advances his theory of the existence of firms. He generalized this by stating (Coase, 1988) that:

> The existence of transaction costs will lead those who wish to trade to engage in practices which bring about a reduction of transaction costs whenever the loss suffered in other ways from the adoption of those practices is less than the transaction costs saved.

Dahlman (1979) described transaction costs as 'search and information costs, bargaining and decision costs, policing and enforcement costs'.

Whilst the initial concept was in terms of trade and the reasons why firms exist, the approach has been transported for analysis of a wide range of economic issues. In particular it has enriched understanding of organizations, both formal and informal and, hence, is relevant to an analysis of the organization and practice of *guanxi*.

Ben-Porath started out by recognizing the numerous transactions costs in exchange. He acknowledged that different transaction costs can have very different behaviour, ranging from one extreme where the transaction cost varies directly with the volume of goods traded to the other extreme where there is only a fixed cost similar to a pure set-up cost. Here Ben-Porath argues that there are some transaction costs that are fixed for fixed trading parties (for variable trading volume). They are like set-up costs for trading with a particular person. He defined the characteristics of such costs[6] as (Ben-Porath 1980):

> Firstly, each person has some stable traits – honesty, reliability, skill, etc. – that interests the other and affects his perception of what he is getting or the terms on which he is getting it. The cost of establishing this mutual view is an investment that facilitates future trading between the parties.

Secondly, the initial establishment of rules and norms regarding the exchange relationship, how each should react to contingencies and dispute settlement is an investment that can benefit all future exchanges.

And, thirdly, there will be a reduction in the chances of cheating because of the expectation of long term gain from repeated exchange.

Because of these characteristics of transaction costs, Ben-Porath put forward his idea that there are advantages in what he calls 'specialization by identity', which means individuals deal only with the same person or with small groups. He contrasted this with the Adam Smith tradition that links specialization and the division of labour to the presence of returns to scale in production. It might be inferred from Ben-Porath's insight that it is meaningless to speak just of specialization alone. There must be specialization in some dimension. For example, a factory may specialize in manufacturing pencils; a distributor may specialize in approaching large buyers of stationery so it is worthwhile to draw goods from various stationery manufacturers, including the pencil manufacturer; a retailer may specialize in consumers of a given locality and it would be worthwhile for him to stock a much greater variety of stationery. So 'at each stage there is a built-in bias toward homogeneity in term of one dimension and heterogeneity in terms of other dimensions'. In the end, 'the balance between specialization by identity and other dimensions derives from the minimization of production and transaction costs and reflects the scale economies connected with the different dimensions' (Ben-Porath, 1980).

Ben-Porath's insights contribute to a theory of *guanxi*. The concept of specialization by identity can be borrowed to analyse behaviour under a *guanxi* regime, which is entirely based on personal identity. His recognition that there has to be stable traits for a specialization by identity to work has to be incorporated into any theory that takes such specialization on board.[7] His recognition of repeated exchange as an enforcement mechanism for specialization by identity is also valuable. However, Ben-Porath's theory is not without its shortcomings if we are thinking of applying it to *guanxi*.

First, though he has given reasons for why specialization by identity can work, he does not give specific situations where specialization by identity solves the problem of organization better (i.e. with lower transaction cost) than other methods (say by resort to the legal system) or where it achieves greater advantage (lower total cost – the sum of transaction cost and production cost) than engaging more in the specialization of other dimensions and sacrificing the lower transaction cost of specialization by identity. That is, he does not engage in a comparative approach. He did try to explain the circumstances when identity is important. However, the descriptions he gave were general descriptions of common transaction costs like uncertainty about quality, uncertainty about contract enforcement, moral hazard and adverse selection for insurance contracts. Other institutions, besides the family or specialization by identity, have been used to minimize such transaction costs. He did not discuss under what circumstances selection by identity would be a more powerful means and under what circumstances it would be less useful.

Second, he gave repeated games as the only constraint on contract enforcement. As will be explained, this method is not a sure-fire way to enforce contracts. In addition, there are a range of other means to enforce contracts to which he did not refer.

Third, no reason is given for why traits should be stable and why the cost of establishing a mutual view of stable traits, as well as the cost involved in the initial establishment of rules and norms regarding exchange relationship, can be low. Though such costs, if low, can facilitate specialization by identity, the identity here can mean an impersonal firm, as well as an individual, so why does Ben-Porath infer that it is the individual person's identity that will be specialized? The establishment of brand names by some companies is also an engagement in specialization by identity and their strategies are also to give the impression of stable traits (in terms of stable quality) and mutual understanding of the way business is to be conducted (in terms of its extending its popularity among potential clients through advertisements and other promotional activities). Impersonal firms can even give customers the impression that these firms are constrained by the benefits of repeated games as customers know that if these firms damage their brand name it will hurt all their future earnings. Ben-Porath does not elaborate on why the identity in his specialization by identity should be personal identity and not firm identity.

The concept of transaction cost is important, but very often, when we move on to real world problems, we have to go into the details and intricacies behind particular situations to understand the specific transaction costs involved as well as to explore the specific methods that are employed to reduce them. Culture, as mental programming, offers a good explanation for why traits are stable and also why specialization by identity in *guanxi* relationships is always personal and not firm-based, and will be discussed in detail later.

Another economic approach using the transaction cost paradigm has been attempted by Landa (1981 and 1983). She specifically targeted the personalized exchange among Chinese middlemen engaged in the marketing of smallholders' rubber in Singapore and West Malaysia in 1969. From her survey she discovered that the real significance of the visible, surface structure of the ethnically homogeneous middleman group lay in its 'underlying deep structure: the invisible codes of ethics, embedded in the personalized exchange relations among its members, which function as constraints against breach of contract and hence facilitate exchange among Chinese middlemen'. She regarded this group as a low-cost club-like institutional arrangement serving as an alternative to contract law and the vertically integrated firm. Landa believed it to have emerged to economize on contract-enforcement and information costs in an environment where the legal infrastructure was not well developed.

Landa's study supports Posner's observation that the transformation of an arm's-length contract relationship into an intimate status relationship is one response to market transaction costs. 'It is a way of bringing reciprocity into the exchange process and thereby increasing the likelihood that promises will be honoured despite the absence of a public enforcement authority' (Posner, 1980).

Landa devised the rank order of relationships shown in Table 2.1 and she equated Confucian ethics as the code of ethics governing

Table 2.1 Landa's grading of social relations

	Categories of social relations	Grade/ranking
A (Insiders)	Near kinsmen from family	1
	Distant kinsmen from extended family	2
	Clansmen	3
	Fellow villagers from China	4
	Fellow Hokkiens	5
	Non-Hokkiens	6
B (Outsiders)	Non-Chinese	7

the group. However, she did not elaborate on the connection between the complexity of Confucian ethics and her simple rank-ordering scheme.

Landa asserted that these relationships have low operating costs because 'the costs of obtaining this valuable input [kinship/ethnic priority rights] is zero for the trading partner possessing a kinship/ethnic status'. She maintained that kinship or ethnic status was not a right that can be purchased. She also maintained that to sort trading partners into the correct category was easy.

This study is valuable because, as far as can be established, it represents the first and to date, the only, attempt by an economist to link Chinese culture, and in particular Confucianism, to trading networks among the Chinese. However, Landa's work suffers from several serious problems.

First, Landa has treated the calculus of relations as the definitive (final) state of relationship between traders. In fact, as referred to previously, this calculus is only what Jacobs (1982) calls the '*guanxi* base'. It should properly be regarded only as a starting point. Trust is not automatically based on the calculus. The subsequent dynamics of *guanxi*, to which Landa makes no reference, is important to the striking of a true *guanxi*. Without analysis of the intricacies behind trading relationships, Landa was only able to offer a very simplified theory, amounting to 'similarity in ethical codes among trading partners means lower transaction cost'.

Similar ethical codes are found in many countries, but have not been used as a substitute for contract law.

Second, Landa has also grossly underestimated the cost of using the group. As she has failed to take into account the dynamics behind *guanxi*, she has missed the costs of developing and maintaining *guanxi*. In addition to her view that one is born into a relationship, other relationships can be developed – at a cost. She thinks that because one is born into a relationship, it is costless but this is not the case and even if one is born into a relationship, there is the need for continued nourishment. Such *guanxi* nourishing activities have brought a lot of business to nightclubs, karaokes, etc.! But one must not take this as bribery, otherwise cash would do a better job!

What is even more significant is the lack of reference to the cost of maintaining the Confucian code of ethics. To be born into a relationship is costless, until we ask the question why some particular relationships entail trust while others do not. Based on Landa, it is because the Confucian code of ethics has dictated that this should be so. Why are agreements within the group easily enforced? Landa believes it must be because the Confucian code of ethics has constrained behaviour. So to be born into certain relationships provides costless trust, and contract enforcement is also not costly. But these views beg the question of 'How costly is it to maintain this Confucian code of ethics which can do these wonderful things?' The answer seems to be that to maintain this code is indeed quite costly. It can be argued that transaction costs have shifted from the devel- -opment of trust and contract enforcement to the maintenance of the Confucian code of ethics. To maintain this code, inculcation has to start early in the life of the person; in the family as well as in school. Discipline has to be maintained to such an extent that for many children creativity is stifled. Various rites and rituals, including paying respect to one's ancestors, have to be performed. On a more general level, the conservatism entailed by Confucian ethics also, arguably, caused China to react inadequately to foreign aggression during the nineteenth and twentieth centuries.[8] Landa's economic study of Chinese trading networks illustrates yet again the problem that economists tend to ignore analysis of cultural dimension.

The theories of *guanxi* or personal networking in business reviewed here are in some ways deficient. However, these ideas, both where they are successful and also where they are unsuccessful have provided valuable insights into how *guanxi* could be better explained and understood.

Culture has to be taken on board. However, the relationship between culture and *guanxi* practice needs to be explained more explicitly. This is partly provided by organizational institutionalists' insights on the reproduction of cultural ideology based on the view that reality is constructed socially. But the reason why one culture and not another culture is adopted has to be explained and the mechanism by which cultural ideology, and so *guanxi* practice, will change has to be identified.

Although the view of institutionalists of the economic approach to network structures in Asia is found wanting, they have challenged all who want to use the choice-theoretic approach to provide a clear and sophisticated exposition of their approach. Users of the choice-theoretic approach are also challenged to explain how misunderstanding of their approach by institutionalists has led to them perceiving problems with the approach when applied to issues that seem to be more social in nature. Also institutionalists' suggestions that the historical dimension should be taken into account is well taken but the lack of any real attempt to do so makes history more their escape clause than a real explanation.

In the case of economic explanations based on the transaction cost paradigm, the problem is one of not getting down to the details of how transaction costs are really being reduced. Their failure to take into account culture or to explain its rationality despite its costly nature has rendered their models severely inadequate.

3 Analysing *guanxi*

The choice-theoretic approach

> Question: How many Chicago school economists are required to change a light bulb?
>
> Answer: None. Because if the light bulb is out and no one has changed it, then this shows that it's probably more efficient to leave the light bulb in its existing state.
>
> (Variation on a joke about free-market economists)

Economics provides the basic guiding assumption for a multidisciplinary approach to *guanxi*; that is, people are selfish and rational and the world is always efficient, or put in economic terms 'people behave according to the postulate of constrained maximization'. In other words, *guanxi* has arisen as a result of the rational choice made by individuals based on their selfish interest so that *guanxi* behaviour is the best approach given the circumstances – this is referred to as a 'choice-theoretic approach to *guanxi*'. The Pareto optimum condition is always satisfied: there is no better way that will benefit some without hurting some others.

If we are to explain something that has happened, then this is the basic condition from which we assess whether the explanation given is adequate. For example, we cannot accept the explanation that *guanxi* is a result of people being influenced by their culture as adequate unless we also explain why adopting this culture is rational and serves the self-interest of individuals subject to constraints.

Constraints in economics

Constraints are all variables that might affect a decision and that are observable. Examples are prices, income, budget, some personal characteristics, existing laws and institutions, available production technology. Everything else is termed a taste, for example, a person's preference for various activities or goods and services (which are unobservable as investigation can only provide very limited information).

(Compiled from: www.carleton.ca/vpac/20000105 (accessed May 2004))

If we are making predictions, we base them on this assumption (given a specification of constraints). When a prediction is not realized, we do not abandon this basic postulate. Instead, we regard the problem as coming from a mistake or insufficiency in the specification of constraints.

Now this may seem counter-intuitive. Wastage and inefficiency seem to be everywhere. For example, people allow tap water to run while brushing their teeth, offer buffet dinners so that diners get more food than they can eat, use time worked to measure output, pollute the air, go to war. However, when we probe deeper, we nearly always find that there is a reason why self-seeking individuals would choose to behave in these ways, given specific constraints. That is, they are rational. Moreover, when we ask the further question of why the constraints are set up in the first place, such constraints also often turn out to be rational, given a wider set of constraints.

But are there any guarantees that whatever exists is efficient? Among the people that we meet everyday, it seems that at least some are often not selfish or rational, and that none are always rational. However, these assumptions are not intended as an accurate description of what the people claim or even honestly think they are doing. As long as this assumption serves our purposes of prediction and explanation, then it should be allowed to stand. We have to caution ourselves against the fallacy of denying the antecedent. Another reason is offered by Alchian (1950) regarding this rationality assumption. It does not matter whether people have clear intentions to be rational or whether they arrive at the efficient behaviour by luck or by calculation. Their mental process is unimportant to economists. What matters is their actual behaviour – the result of that mental process. As long as there is scarcity, all inefficient behaviour will be eliminated by competition and only efficient behaviour survives.

Economics – contrasts

Wisdom arising from economics:

> The key to doing well lies not in overcoming others but in eliciting their co-operation. Individuals don't have to be rational; the evolutionary process alone allows the successful strategy to thrive, even if the players do not know why or how. Finally, no central authority is needed; co-operation based on reciprocity can be self-policing.
>
> (Robert Axelrod)

And some facetious views:

> An economist is a man who states the obvious in terms of the incomprehensible.
>
> (Alfred A. Knopf)

> If all economists were laid end to end, they would not reach a conclusion.
>
> (George Bernard Shaw)

> Economics is extremely useful as a form of employment for economists.
>
> (John Kenneth Galbraith)
>
> (Compiled from:www.quotationspage.com, www.meister.u-net.com/economics/quotations_ee.htm (accessed May 2004))

This evolutionary view of efficiency has been disputed by many economists. One problem is that for adaptation to occur there has to be diversity, trial and error. That means, at each point in time, there will be in existence some arrangements, methods or products which will not actually work and so will not survive in the long run. However no matter how short the time during which they are in existence, the important point is that they do exist for some time. So some phenomena that we observe might not be efficient. The second problem is that 'time is also required for the most efficient method to evolve'.[1] For example, a firm sees new opportunities due to a change in the environment. It will take some time for the firm to make preparations to capture this new opportunity, say in making investments, employing the necessary expertise, and so on. Third, some methods might have evolved to adapt to a particular situation at a given point in time and be the best fit for that time. However, as the environment changes, this particular arrangement may not be the best fit for the new situation. Thus, the person or society is locked into a 'local-maxima', which is less efficient than the 'global-maxima'. The QWERTY keyboard[2] or the technologically inferior Disk Operating System (DOS) of Microsoft are examples. People become so used to these designs that it is very difficult to switch to better ones.

These views seem to have ignored the fundamental economic problem of scarcity. We are limited in our abilities, resources and time. Take the first objection. If we are not omniscient, then trial and error and the existence of seemingly inefficient arrangements are necessary costs for the generation of diversity, which will benefit the continued fit of the whole of society. So society, taken as a whole, is efficient. It is utopian to imagine that even after eliminating inefficient elements from society, it can still survive in the same way. A search party of 100 policemen is sent to rescue a hiker lost in the hills but if only one policeman finds the hiker it cannot be said that the effort of the other 99 policemen is a waste and that only the policeman who found the hiker should have been sent. The effort of the other 99 policemen is part of the necessary costs of the rescue operation. This is a cost we have to pay for the scarcity of information (of where the hiker is).

The objection that time is required for a movement towards an efficient situation, so before this is achieved the situation is inefficient, ignores the cost of rapid adaptation. It is a technical limitation. Resources are not perfectly malleable. It is thus a necessary cost that time is required for adaptation. Now if the situation at a given point in time seems not to be the ending point, this does not mean that the situation is not efficient. When the cost of moving towards the ending point is considered, the inefficiency conclusion may be seem to be the result of ignoring the constraint of the extremely high cost of instant adaptation.

Now we come to the objection that there are situations where a mere local-maxima is reached that has prevented the world from moving to a global maxima. Looking more closely at the QWERTY keyboard example, since we are now fully aware of the irrationality of the keyboard, why is it that we do not change to a keyboard that is easier to learn? The inertia in this resistance to move towards a better situation results from the fact that so many people are familiar with the QWERTY keyboard and various arrangements (both institutional and technological) are already geared towards this keyboard. To switch to a new keyboard means that additional costs are required which are not justifiable by the gain in doing so. So if we take this switching cost into account, to stick to the QWERTY keyboard is an efficient response and this keyboard is now the global maximum, not just a local one.

One might argue that it is efficient for us to stick to the QWERTY keyboard but how about all the future generations which have not learnt the keyboard at all? But if the gain from all these future generations is so great why has someone not introduced a revolutionary keyboard to capture this gain? There might be two answers to this. First the gain from future generations is uncertain because an even more revolutionary input method might come about replacing the keyboard altogether, for example, input by voice. Second, there are difficulties for manufacturers of a revolutionary keyboard to capture the gain enjoyed by its introduction. The first answer amounts to saying that the gain, because of its uncertain nature, is not great enough to justify the cost of switching. The second answer is basically an externalities argument; the problem of external benefits (that is benefits accruing to those not directly involved in developing and manufacturing the keyboard) causes the underproduction of this revolutionary keyboard. Now if we take into consideration the costs of rectifying the problem of externalities, say in tampering with property rights structures, then again the total costs in so doing may not justify the potential gains of switching. The QWERTY keyboard seems an unimportant example but issues about language and culture have characteristics very similar to the QWERTY keyboard.

So to summarize, the general argument about the local maxima/global maxima issue is that if we are aware of the value differential between the two maxima and if we still stick to the local maxima because the cost of switching to the global maxima is too high, then the local maxima should be considered as the new global maxima because it is the maxima after considering all costs and benefits. If we are not even aware of the global maxima, then the question is: does it exist? Or to put it in another way, ignorance represents an uncertain but potentially high cost of switching.

A defence of the evolutionary view of efficiency is important because this view is adopted in arguing in favour of the choice-theoretic approach in dealing with culture. In this regard, culture has to be understood to be efficient. However one important characteristic (and value) of culture is its persistence. With persistence, adaptation of culture to change in the environment is slow and so the above arguments against evolutionary efficiency might seem valid objections to the efficiency of culture. It is against this way of thinking that the above defence is directed.

The debate of the rationality assumption still continues and the issue in not put to rest by the above arguments. However, they are considered to be sufficient in justifying its use in analysing *guanxi*.

The implication of adopting the choice-theoretic approach in explaining *guanxi* means that it will establish the constraints that have given rise to *guanxi* behaviour as a rational response. Then to go one step further, these constraints themselves will in turn be explained by being shown also to be maximizing.

A multidisciplinary analysis

My basic attitude towards these disciplinary distinctions is that they are pointless, boring, unproductive and indeed counterproductive. Both the best and most interesting work is often done by people who could not care less about where they come from (Jon Elster in Swedberg, 1990).

The choice-theoretic approach with the maximization postulate as the guiding assumption is the basis for analysing *guanxi*. So why not stick to a totally economic inquiry of *guanxi*? Well, in fact, economists have done very little research on the subject, probably due to their strong tendency to deal with issues that can easily be formalized into a more abstract language – mathematics. As noted by Olsen (1968):

> And where economic theory is not in itself deficient, economists often are: they sometimes lack the fullness of mind, the judgment, and, above all, the imagination needed to apply economic theory to problems outside their traditional purview.

A multidisciplinary approach is especially important for studying social institutions. Acheson (1992), an institutional economist noted:

> Economists seem to be oblivious to what is happening in psychology, philosophy, sociology and anthropology. Anthropologists and sociologists, for their part, are largely unaware

that economists have done any work on the generation of institutions, much less have any idea about the analytical insights they have developed.

Although the choice-theoretic approach has been adopted, insights from other disciplines, including anthropology, sociology, organizational theory, Chinese philosophy, Chinese history, epistemology and law, are drawn upon. How these different insights are to be integrated into a coherent, organic whole will emerge in this and the next chapter. Suffice to say here that *guanxi* has distinctive Chinese cultural elements, so work by anthropologists and sociologists are illuminating. Chinese culture is closely related to Chinese philosophy which, unlike Western philosophy, is more a practical philosophy on how one should lead one's life, so it will give clues to what Chinese culture actually implies. To understand why this philosophy is accepted by the people and sanctioned by the state, an understanding of Chinese history is essential. If culture is treated as part of the stock of knowledge and theory about the world of a people, then to understand how this stock of knowledge and theory is formed and changed will require an understanding of epistemology. As will become evident later, *guanxi* serves as an alternative to contract law. So how is it able to achieve that and why is law not used instead? An understanding of law throws some light on the issue. *Guanxi* has also been able to help relate firms or individuals to each other, so it is a form of organization and studies by organizational theorists will be useful.

A multidisciplinary approach is never easy but is necessary to draw the best from different disciplines in order to explain *guanxi*. However, when faced with their widely differing assumptions, methodology, style of presentation, and concerns, the task is formidable. It is more than the simple task of juxtaposing what everyone is saying about the what, how and why of *guanxi* (and related issues). It requires an attempt to form a dialogue between the disciplines and to make a judgement – a give and take decision – of whether and how each piece from each discipline is to be used in the explanation. To overcome this difficulty the maximization postulate is taken as the foundation for the explanatory structure.

This will then become the centre around which insights from various disciplines revolve.

The *guanxi* puzzle

Given our basic postulate of maximizing individuals, the most puzzling aspects of *guanxi* is that it makes the two parties to an agreement less reliant on the sanction of law for its enforcement. This problem of voluntary cooperation has intrigued people for a very long time. The obligation for mutual exchange of favours can be understood as an implicit agreement to provide a sort of insurance to the other party. This is an agreement to exchange because both parties expect to offer help when asked and both would try to repay the *renqing* debt at some later date and is an exchange without the sanction of law.

Game theory in economics

Game theory is a formal way to analyse interactions amongst a group of rational agents who behave strategically.

This definition contains a number of important concepts:

Group: in any game there is more than one decision maker who is referred to as a player. If there is only one player it becomes a decision problem.

Interaction: what one individual other player does affects at least one other player in the group. Otherwise the game is simply a series of independent decision problems.

Strategic: individual players account for this interdependence.

Rational: whilst accounting for this interdependence each player chooses his or her best action.

(Compiled from: http://www.courses.fas.harvard.edu/~ec1052/lecture/lecture1.pdf, (accessed May 2004))

Cooperation is not always a puzzle. For example, if non-cooperation is not beneficial to all parties, it is only natural for self-seeking individuals to cooperate. However, this is trivial. What is most intriguing, and not trivial, is the problem of voluntary cooperation as illustrated by the prisoner's dilemma. In this game there are two players, A and B. It might be assumed that they are two business-men who have just struck an agreement. Say both agree not to cut their prices further in selling their flats in a particular location. Now each has two choices, to cooperate or to defect. To cooperate means that they abide by their agreement, while to defect means to go back on one's word. Table 3.1 illustrates the payoff to each party for different combinations of choices.

Now the interesting thing about this game is that no matter what B chooses to do (and whether A knows about B's final decision or not), it always seems rational for A to defect – what game theorists call the dominant strategy. The reasoning is this: if B cooperates, then A can get $2 more by defecting. If B defects, then A can get $1 more by defecting. So no matter what B does, A will get a higher payoff by defecting. The problem is that B will follow the same reasoning as the case is symmetrical so B will defect too. Since both A and B will defect, the end result will be: A gets $1 and B gets $1. An example occurred in Hong Kong in mid-1998 when Henderson Land and Nan Fung Properties agreed with each other not to cut flat prices in Junk Bay (Tseung Kwan O). The agreement broke down

Table 3.1 The prisoner's dilemma

		Player B	
		Cooperate	Defect
Player A	Cooperate	A gets $3 B gets $3 (Mutual cooperation)	A gets $0 B gets $5 (Sucker's payoff, and temptation to defect)
	Defect	A gets $5 B gets $0 (Sucker's payoff, and temptation to defect)	A gets $1 B gets $1 (Punishment for mutual defection)

in August 1998 when Nan Fung began cutting prices. The issue led to some public animosity between the two developers.

So it seems that it is not easy for cooperation to occur. Agreeing to cooperate is easy. However, if the depiction of the prisoner's dilemma is accurate, then people will always go back on their word, so actual cooperation is hard to come by.

Now the problem for A and B is that the defect/defect combination yields the lowest total payoff. This is only natural because cooperation is supposed to bring benefits so the fruits of cooperation will not be bestowed upon those who do not cooperate.

The most pessimistic answer to the problem of cooperation between selfish people was given over 300 years ago by Thomas Hobbes (1651/1962). He offered only two alternatives. One alternative was that we submit all our liberty to an all-powerful government – the 'Leviathan'. Otherwise, we shall enter a state of nature where selfish people compete with each other so ruthlessly that life would be 'solitary, poor, nasty, brutish, and short'. So for him, not only is law required but also the government has also to be all powerful in order that people would cooperate to make life better for all. Now the puzzle in explaining *guanxi* is that such a central enforcer is not required.

Before we move on to offer an explanation of *guanxi*'s ability to make voluntary cooperation without law possible, it is necessary to delve into what is behind the prisoner's dilemma formulation. The maximization postulate is the cornerstone of the explanation of *guanxi* yet the prisoner's dilemma outcome seems to pose the first challenge to this postulate because if one looks at all four possible outcomes, one is struck by the apparent irrationality of the equilibrium outcome. The total payoff is the least if both defect. Also, there is at least one outcome, the cooperate/cooperate combination, where both parties will be better off than the present predicament and yet this is not chosen according to game theory.

To counter this challenge to the postulate of maximization, we must go behind the prisoner's dilemma formulation and understand the rules. The answer might become apparent if we consider this: given the prospect of the rather unfavourable outcome, would it not be to both parties' benefit to find a solution so that the payoff to both parties can be increased? So what is preventing such a solution? The problem (again) does not lie in agreeing to a solution but to the way both parties commit to their promise. Put in economic terms, there is an extremely high transaction cost in enforcing the agreement. Expressed in this way, the defect/defect outcome is rational after all, given such a high transaction cost. To move to cooperate/cooperate, does not justify the cost paid for enforcing the commitment.

It is tempting to say that the prisoner's dilemma formulation has given an apparently irrational result because it has assumed that there is no communication between 'prisoners'. That is, information cost is assumed to be infinite. In real life situations information can very often be exchanged, so this extreme assumption does not hold. What is more, as mentioned in the earlier example, A's choice is independent of his knowledge about what B will choose. So even if there is perfect knowledge, both will defect. The misconception of taking high information cost as the culprit behind the game is probably due to the original story used to illustrate it; that of two prisoners separately interrogated.

Because of analogies recognized between games of strategy and forms of economic and political cooperation, game theory has attracted considerable attention within the social sciences. Some game theory practitioners have tried to use game theory to account for the emergence of certain institutions. However, a different line of attack is developed here. The reason is that, for the student of institutions, the major value of game theory lies in its apparent power to elucidate the consequences of institutional variation. As for why those institutions have come about in the first place, there seems not much game theory can offer.

A precondition for the conduct of an analysis by game theory of the organization of economic, political and social life is the specification of the game's fundamental rules. For the analysis of such activities by game theory, the rules of the game are defined by the environment within which they take place. Here we attempt to explain why the fundamental rules of *guanxi* have come about in the first place.

To go back to the apparent irrationality of the defect/defect outcome, we have explained why this would be rational given extreme enforcement costs. However, it is certainly to everyone's advantage to lower enforcement costs so generating a possible gain. This is achieved by moving to cooperate/cooperate, thus altering the rules of the game and transforming it. It seems that *guanxi* has done this job well and it is the task of the next chapter to speculate on the reasons why.

The apparent violation of the postulate of maximization can be explained thus: either the prisoner's dilemma outcome is rational because of the prohibitively high transaction cost of instituting enforcement mechanisms for contracts of cooperation, or the outcome is not the actual outcome, because the high transaction cost assumed by the game is not valid.

Guanxi technology

The puzzling thing about *guanxi* is that the sanction of the law or the state is not sought when businessmen engage in commercial transactions. It is argued that the reason is to reduce the various transaction costs in business and that, among the various transaction costs, the focus of the reduction is the cost of contract enforcement. To achieve contract enforcement *guanxi* involves elaborate techniques which are referred to here as *guanxi* technology and include the *guanxi* base, *guanxi* reference, *renqing*, social interactions, personal relationship, and totality of the relationship, repeated transactions and face.

Such technology is viable largely because of the constraints of Chinese culture and has developed in the specific context of the long history of China's method of social control. A number of characteristics of the *guanxi* relationship in action have been noted and their technical aspects are examined here to see why some of them have served the purpose of reducing the reliance on legal enforcement. Later chapters consider the influence of the two most important components of this social control; the state ideology, which is also responsible for a large part of China's culture, and the legal system adopted by most of the dynasties since Han

(206 BC to 220 AD). The rationality of adopting this unique method of social control will in turn be explained.

Guanxi base

A *guanxi* base determines the ease with which *guanxi* can actually be developed. It is the starting point of *guanxi* not an end. The base could include what Jacobs (1982) has cited; family, kinship, hometown, classmates, co-workers. Landa (1981, 1983) tried to present various 'categories of sameness'. Though, an absolute classification is not possible, by identifying two generic sources of the base we might be able to gain some clues as to the rationale behind different categories. The first source is prescriptive; one is born into that relationship base. They include kinship, same hometown village, and same dialect. Another category is achieved; they are developed later in life, though there is no implication that the base is deliberately developed. Such categories include classmates, schoolmates, co-workers, teacher-student, and superior–subordinate. That the achieved relationship is not deliberately developed is important because a deliberate push for a relationship would lower its credibility. It is however interesting to note that there is no lack of deliberate intentions to develop a superior *guanxi* base by parents who want to do all they can to get their sons or daughters into prestigious schools in Hong Kong. The actual friendships struck between the students themselves are of course not deliberate. Moreover, the deliberation on the part of the parents would not lower much the credibility of this *guanxi* base because the fact that they are successful in their attempt to put their children into these schools indicates the amount of resources available to them and this is a good proxy for their own worth as a connection for others in this *guanxi* base!

The power of *guanxi* technology

Two extracts from an article by Morgen Witzel, deputy editor of *Mastering Management Online*, and co-author of *Doing Business*

continued

in China (Routledge, 2000), illustrate some benefits of *guanxi* on the world economic stage:

A natural affinity for alliances

Whether, as many claim, this stems from Confucian culture or from a more general desire to avoid conflict if necessary, Chinese managers tend to choose alliances and partnerships as a natural means of achieving growth and expansion. On the whole, they tend to be better at this than Western companies. This is not to say alliances in China do not fail – they do, often – but Chinese companies are far more likely to go on looking for the right partner than give up and go it alone.

The role of the overseas Chinese

In dealing with these problems, China does hold an ace card: the overseas Chinese community. Some 60m people of Chinese descent live outside the country, mainly in south-east Asia – the most important concentrations being in Malaysia, Singapore, Thailand, Indonesia and the Philippines – but with other communities scattered around the world, especially in the US. These people and the businesses they own and work represent a powerful economic force: according to one estimate in the late 1990s, if they were a country in their own right, they would have a GDP two-thirds the size of that of Japan.

The biggest overseas Chinese companies – Cheung Kong, Kerry Everbright, CP Group and others – are also among the largest investors in China itself. Over the past decades these overseas Chinese companies have been a natural conduit for Chinese companies acquiring not only investment but also technology and skills.

Relations between overseas Chinese and their cousins in the People's Republic of China are not always smooth: despite their common Chinese heritage there are some cultural differences, and there are cases of the latter group refusing to work with or for overpaid 'foreigners' from Singapore or Malaysia. Nevertheless, since the beginning of the economic reform movement the overseas Chinese have played a very important role in that movement. Now, with their high technology, strong management skills and worldwide trading and finance connections, they look set to play an equally important role in assisting Chinese companies to expand overseas.

(Source: www.ftmastering.com/mmo/mmo10_1.htm (accessed May 2004))

The reason for an initial reliance on a *guanxi* base is that it is an efficient way to limit who we should do business with. The reason is two-fold. First, the similarity presupposes some mutual understanding; the character of the person, the family background, the environment within which one grows up, the language that one speaks. For achieved similarities, besides the implied background similarity which has brought different people together, as in the case of classmates or co-workers, there is the further mutual understanding of the very personal ways of expression and more efficient communication due to the long time spent living or working together. The *guanxi* base is also a reference network through which we could more easily ask about what others think about a potential business associate. Now this mutual understanding would be valueless in a world with no transaction cost, in particular with no information cost about the quality of goods and services. However, if goods and services cannot be evaluated easily, then an understanding of how a business partner would normally act is important in assessing the risk of a deal. This is crucial in the case where binding contracts are not available to govern that the quality of the goods and services supplied conforms to the original agreement. There is an implicit assumption that our characters constrain our behaviour and our characters cannot be changed easily. Moreover, pretending to be one kind of person while we are in fact another sort of person is costly (Frank, 1987, 1988).

Also, the *guanxi* base increases the opportunity cost of breaking agreements. If one side to the agreement violates some mutual understanding about each party's obligations, what is damaged is probably not only the relationship between the two persons, but also the relationships between the agreement breaker and other members within their *guanxi* base.

Guanxi reference

If one (say A) is not within the *guanxi* base of B, A could ask someone who has *guanxi* with both A and B to act as an introducer. This introducer is not free of any obligations on A's behaviour towards B. If A cheats B, B would blame the introducer too. Now this constrains the introducer to be careful in providing references. In a way, he serves as a third party guarantor or enforcer of the agreement between A and B. But would the introducer have any incentive to provide references then? The answer is positive because this is a favour that he gives to A and a repayment would be expected. Any deals struck between A and B also means that B has benefited and so he would also be indebted to the introducer. So there are risks but also rewards for providing references.

Rules of propriety

Respectfulness, without the rules of propriety, becomes laborious bustle; carefulness, without the rules of propriety, becomes timidity; boldness, without the rules of propriety, becomes insubordination; straightforwardness, without the rules of propriety, becomes rudeness.

(Confucius)

Renqing

Renqing rules define the propriety of behaviour. Such elaborate rules might be regarded by non-Chinese (and even Chinese) as rather tiresome and unnecessary. However, it provides the two parties with the certainty of the relationship. There is certainty of what each move means. The willingness to take the trouble to adhere to the rules conveys the meaning of good intentions. The ability to conduct oneself according to the rules also gives certainty as to the ease of communication with this person in future. Moreover, the *renqing* rules are not precise rules that one can apply mechanically. It takes a lot of training and practice so that one can conduct oneself in a way that can be regarded as smooth. There are no formal schools for this. All training and practice comes from business experience in the Chinese cultural context. *Chang xiu shan wu* denotes a person who is able to conduct his business relationship as if in a dance. This implicit meaning is that he is a successful businessman. *Mian mian qu yuan* means a person is able to take care of his relationships with others without offending anyone. There is in Chinese the phrase *renqing shigu,* which means worldly wisdom. So the ability to conduct oneself in *renqing* as if it is second nature denotes that the businessman is up to the level where the two can talk business. This is a very important screening device.

Renqing rules limit the number of responses but improve efficiency, mainly in terms of speed of the communication because quite complicated meanings can be conveyed through certain rituals. In this way, the rules are more like rules of language.

Social interactions and entertainment

To develop *guanxi*, social interactions are required. Very often this is by way of going out for entertainment together. Usually one party acts as host and the other as party guest. Going to banquets or nightclubs together has been interpreted by some as bribery, or if it is the client that is being entertained, then it is interpreted as a kind of favour to solicit business. However, if it is just bribery or a favour, why the hassle? Why not pay cash instead, or in the case of the client, why not lower the price instead? Payment in kind is wasteful and if it is in the form of entertainment, the 'payment' cannot be resold for any value. Additionally, it is not only cash that the host must pay, he also has to spend long hours with his guest and time is usually costly for a businessman. So the bribery/favour interpretation is not satisfactory or at least not the whole story.

In a world where information is scarce, spending the evening together at a social event is a great opportunity to develop mutual understanding. To know the character of one's business associate is always an important part of the training of a Chinese entrepreneur. For example, deducing the trustworthiness of a person from his facial features – physiognomy – is one aspect of such training. It is during such informal periods that one's true self is revealed simply because it is more difficult to hide. Conversation is likely to be about various aspects of business, family or other things of personal concern. This allows the parties to know much about each other's background, character and responses in different situations before embarking on their business deal. Behaviour in an unstructured environment provides more information about how risky a deal is. In such a setting it is, of course, possible to refrain from saying anything about oneself but this means that *guanxi* will be much more difficult to develop.

There is also the possibility that the two can develop true friendship and in that case there is an added element of emotion-affection in the relationship as a guarantee for enforcement. Having an enjoyable time together definitely provides one such chance for friendship to develop. However, even if this is not achieved, and it is not usually supposed to be the major aim, such occasions serve to lower the cost of obtaining information about one's opposite number.

As noted by Akerlof (1983), Frank (1988) and Becker (1976) in their analysis of seemingly 'irrational' behaviour such as altruism, honesty, and being genuinely nice to others, social interaction is vital for the long-term survival of such 'irrational' behaviour, thus making such behaviour 'rational' after all! It is through social interaction that such 'irrational' characteristics are made known to others who wish to cooperate with such 'irrational' yet wonderful people rather than with others who are 'rational' and so, selfish. Such a reaction would thus benefit persons with such 'irrational' characteristics.

The numerous informal social interactions common to Chinese *guanxi* building provide exactly this chance. By this means a person possessing Chinese cultural characteristics such as concern for relationships with others and abhorrence of confrontation will be made known to others.

Furthermore, the various ways to increase mutual knowledge is in fact one kind of investment specificity (Williamson, 1985). That is, such investment is good only for trading with that particular business associate. If you want to trade with another person, this investment will be useless and the process of getting to know about each other has to start all over again. So having achieved a certain degree of mutual knowledge, there is less tendency to change the business relationship. A lock-in is established. What is more, the willingness to engage in this investment when no material reward has yet been committed conveys a credible intention to trade.

Guanxi as always personal

A further important characteristic of *guanxi* is that it is always personal. It is always struck between two persons. Even if the business is ostensibly between two firms it is understood that the business is really between the two persons or, what amounts to the same thing, the deal is guaranteed by the two persons. The implication is that the person is always personally liable for any breach of the agreement between the two firms. This inability to shift responsibilities from the person, usually the patriarch, increases the opportunity cost of taking risks and cheating. This makes both parties more cautious because what is at stake is not just the particular deal but also deals in future. It works in a similar manner to the unlimited liability of a sole proprietor. One can bankrupt a limited liability company and start all over again but liabilities with the person terminate only at death.

The totality of the relationship

A further characteristic of *guanxi* is that it is not possible to separate the different roles each person has with the other. For example, when doing business with a close friend special treatment will be given. Each party will not treat the other in the same way as when they do business with any businessman. That is, it is not possible to change one's treatment of the other according to the requirement of each role. The interpretation of *shu huan shu, lu huan lu* (business is business and should not be intermingled with other aspects of our relationship), as showing the ability of the Chinese to separate their behaviour when acting in different roles (for example King, 1991) is inappropriate. In an environment where a mechanism to guarantee contract enforcement is lacking, the Chinese have allowed the borrowing of the trust previously built up between two persons, say because of the mutual understanding and affection developed when they were colleagues, to lower the risk of agreement enforcement when the two strike a business deal. This would not be possible if each has an expectation that when doing business, the previous friendship does not count. In fact, when your 'friend' says *shu huan shu, lu huan lu* to you, he is in fact saying that 'our friendship is not close enough to warrant special favours' and fair treatment is upheld instead to cover up the embarrassment of not granting this favour.

This means that if the good relationship previously established is put up as collateral and the business does not work out as expected, then the previous relationship will be damaged. Not all Chinese are willing to risk a good relationship as collateral. They are perfectly aware of the risk and that is why people may refrain from doing business with kinsmen or friends altogether because the collateral is too high a price to pay for the small gain from business. Neither are they willing to say *shu huan shu, lu huan lu* because it is really difficult, within the Chinese cultural context, to say this without implying that 'we are not really that close'.

The Chinese cultural context makes it very difficult to convey the meaning that there are a number of abstract roles and that when one is treating the other in a particular way, it is just acting out of the responsibility of one of these roles and that nothing is implied about the relationship in other roles. To be able to separate the different roles one has with another person may have its advantages in other cultures. However, if, as in a Chinese context, there are no credible enforcement mechanisms for business deals, it is worthwhile to give up these niceties!

Repeated transactions

In the process of building up *guanxi*, the two parties will probably start to trade in small quantities. The trading volume or the extent of cooperation will increase with time. This is a cautious way to test the other person's reliability, as the small quantity traded in the initial stage makes the risk to the business small. There is also very little incentive to cheat. Further repeated trading makes such trade smoother as each becomes more used to the other's way of doing business. Physical resources might even be modified to facilitate trading with this *guanxi* party. The benefit (or rent, in economic terms) generated by such mutual adjustment increases the opportunity cost of terminating the relationship. Furthermore, when the two trading parties have developed long term and intensive trading relationships, then a break-up will be very traumatic. In a way, the rent from familiarity is a form of collateral for the continuation of the relationship.

Also, the prospect of cumulative gains from a series of future trading activities increases the opportunity cost of defaulting on agreements. This is what game theorists regard as the repeated game case. One common argument raised to counter the repeated game argument for cooperation as in Axelrod (1984) goes like this:

> Even for repeated games, the cooperation must somehow end one day. Then there is no longer any time left to punish the defector by withdrawing future cooperation. So on this last move, there will be no future to consider, and the dominant strategy is to cheat. But if the worst result is to be expected for this last round, then strategy for the penultimate game will not depend on consideration for this last game. So this penultimate game effectively becomes the last one to consider. Once again, defection is the dominant strategy and the reasoning is the same as was applied to the last game. This chain of argument will work its way step by step backwards until it

reaches the first round. So ultimately, even for this first round, the dominant strategy is to cheat.

However, this argument can be countered in a number of ways: the exact ending round of trade is not certain; trading volume is small; if it so happens that the opposite number is a nice guy who will not cheat in the last game, then for the selfish guy to cheat in the first game is very costly; present gain has a much higher present value than the cost of the breakdown of cooperation in future (based mainly on Dixit and Nalebuff, 1991).

Face

Face (*mianzi*) is an integral part of Chinese culture and *guanxi* dynamics. The Chinese are most concerned about their face. Apart from explaining this by saying that it is a special characteristic of the Chinese, which amounts to abdicating from any economic explanation, it can be interpreted as a measurement of the respect others are willing to give a person. The fact that so many people are willing to give face to someone means that this person is not held in low esteem by at least this many people.

Face and social obligations

Ray, a Chinese journalist in the office where I worked in Hong Kong was leaving to emigrate. The office staff booked a room in a restaurant to give him a farewell dinner, then divided the bill among themselves. But because of the big disparities in earnings in Hong Kong, some of the better-paid staff members suggested that the lower earners be exempt from sharing the cost of the meal. A sharp-witted Chinese secretary put her foot down at once, saying, 'You cannot do that. It is their face towards Ray.'

(Bonavia, 1980)

On occasions such as a son's marriage, it is vital that as many people as possible give face and attend the banquet. This is especially so for those in the business sector. The occasion presents a rare chance for a public display of one's network. This display has several implications. First, a substantial network is one of the most important assets for a businessman. To let others know that one has such a network increases other people's incentive to build up *guanxi* with you because doing so provides them with potential access to many other people. Second, a large network again serves as collateral for trade with any one person. The whole network can break down upon the discovery of dishonesty on only one occasion. It works much like a brand name. Because the brand name is so valuable in its own right, the brand owner will not easily allow the brand to be damaged. In turn, the consumers' confidence in the quality of the good is boosted due to high opportunity cost to the brand owner if he cheats. The same situation holds for face in *guanxi*. If a person has a lot of face, this increases the opportunity cost of cheating and loss of face. This in turn increases the trading partner's confidence in trading with this person.

Face – China vs the West

(By Westerners) face is commonly viewed as a kind of conceit or vanity, a desire never to be seen as stupid or wrong headed. As such it runs against the Western/Christian tradition of admitting one's mistakes and trying to do better in future.

Face is a more complex concept than this. It is an unwritten set of rules by which people in society cooperate to avoid unduly damaging each other's prestige and self-respect. Naturally, people implacably hostile to one another may refuse to cooperate in this way and will do whatever they can to make each other lose face . . . but in relationships which are only mildly antagonistic – for instance in bargaining for a business deal each side expects the other to take his or her face into account. Thus if a hard bargain is struck, and one party seems to have suffered a tactical defeat, the winning party should make some token concessions to save the other's face. Both sides and possibly

continued

some onlookers, know exactly who has won or lost in the actual bargaining, but the loser has also won a kind of minor moral victory by eliciting sufficient respect from the winner to qualify for a face saving arrangement.

The idea of being a good loser, considered important in Western ethics, is replaced by being a good winner in Chinese ethics – not rubbing one's victory in or crowing over it.

The importance of face in China helps to smooth out ruffled personal relations between Chinese and foreigners, because the Chinese will be pleased with a face saving gesture, whereas it will mean little to the European to make it.

(Bonavia, 1980)

Guanxi technology revisited

Without the constraint of transaction costs *guanxi* technologies would become wasteful and irrational. A *guanxi* base is not a perfect way to screen potential trading partners. It is only used as a proxy in lieu of a better way for initial selection. There might well be other more trustworthy or more competent trading partners. If there is no transaction cost, then to favour say a relative who is not very competent over an unrelated person who is more competent is irrational and wasteful. However, when there is no low cost way to ascertain trustworthiness, the risk involved in trading with a stranger can translate into a high transaction cost that prevents the trade occurring. Now this is rational.

The other *guanxi* technologies can all be interpreted in this light. The need for *guanxi* reference, the following of the rather rigid rules of *renqing*, the spending of resources on long hours of entertainment, the lumping of all business risks onto the individual, the making of a *guanxi* relationship the totality of the relationship, the gradual nature of the growth of trade between parties, the elaborate and sometimes costly way to maintain and demonstrate face are all costly and irrational to engage in were there not transaction costs.

Further evidence lends support to the above premise. In research reports on firm size and scope in Hong Kong and Taiwan two features stand out; firms in Hong Kong and Taiwan are relatively smaller than in other regions and there is a tendency for Chinese businessmen to have a wide scope of business (see for example Redding and Tam (1985), Myers (1982) and Zhao (1982)).

Business in East Asia

Business in East Asia is neither an art nor a science. It is a practice. Timely and accurate basic data are unavailable. *Guanxi, xinyong, renqing, mianzi*, corruption, fluid regulations are prevalent. Business is also cultural and communication biased, and communication is 75 percent nonverbal. In fact, emotional communication is 90 percent nonverbal, therefore only first-hand learning in Asia teaches us how to take action, and gain cooperation from others to achieve results.

(Dr Wong Yip Yan, Founder and Chairman of the WyWy Group of Companies)

The characteristics of *guanxi* determine that the business owner is neither able to transfer his *guanxi* network in total nor delegate the handling of *guanxi* to another person, although it is accepted that a small part can be 'lent' or transferred by way of acting as *guanxi* reference for another person. In a world where *guanxi* is a person's major competitive edge, the business owner becomes a really busy man having to develop and maintain the *guanxi* network himself. His time, as well as his mental and physical strength, sets the limit to the expansion of his business.

Employees who have the chance to develop their own *guanxi* network will tend to break away from their original firm. This tendency to break away is one reason for the relatively small size of firms. Because a *guanxi* network is always personal, setting up one's own firm is the best way to capture the value of this network. Selling the connections to one's employer is not an option.

The tendency of Chinese businessmen to engage in a wide scope of business is also consistent with the nature of *guanxi* as the trust developed by various *guanxi* is a fixed factor that can be shared by different kinds of trade. It is not like economies of scale of the technological kind where the facility can only be shared by production of the same kind of good. When the fixed factor is the trust and *guanxi* of the person, it does not matter what sort of goods are traded. This is what is known as specialization by identity (Ben-Porath, 1980).

There is therefore a tendency for the entrepreneurs to maximize the value of the trust they have developed by dealing in as many types of goods as possible. Of course, other technological economies and diseconomies prevent the entrepreneur from unlimited expansion of the scope of his or her business but the economies of using *guanxi* will result in a range of business wider than economies where such specialization by identity is less important.

4 The influence of Chinese culture

It seems obvious that the workings of *guanxi* technology display distinctly Chinese characteristics. This is why many scholars have related *guanxi* to Chinese culture. But the perspective taken here prefers to characterize the relationship of *guanxi* with Chinese culture in terms of Chinese culture being a constraint on *guanxi* behaviour. This way of putting it might seem paradoxical because *guanxi* is supposed to enable the Chinese to conduct business without the sanction of contract law, yet a constraint is supposed to disable some choice, that is to limit the choices available. However, this will not appear so paradoxical if one recognizes that law is doing exactly the same thing. It is a device to enable less risky trade by subordinating everyone to its rules. In fact, Hobbes's radical solution follows the same formula: give up all your freedom to the Leviathan and you are at least free to live peacefully together.

Before moving on, it might be worthwhile to dismiss two issues which might pose obstacles to the explanation of the way culture has constrained *guanxi* behaviour. First, it has been noted by various researchers that to enforce agreements using particularistic relationships rather than contract law is not unique to the Chinese. It is not uncommon in other cultures, including Western cultures, to have agreements without the sanction of law. So would it then follow that culture is not important in the explanation? The contention here is that there is no logical ground to dismiss the constraint of Chinese culture simply based on such evidence. There is an especially widespread use of personal relationships among the

Chinese and there is uniqueness in the Chinese way of using personal relationships. In fact, these might be reasons why the word *guanxi* is used to describe the Chinese case instead of the more general term 'personal or particularistic ties'.

Another point concerns the argument that mainstream economics has used against cultural explanations: that culture, as an explanation, is either tautological or incomplete because culture itself has to be explained. The tautology argument comes about because some definitions of culture are so broad that any human behaviour can be explained as culture. However, the argument here differs from mainstream economics in the way that these problems are dealt with. Instead of evading cultural explanations altogether, as is often the case in mainstream economics, here we seek to improve them.

With regard to the problem of tautology, a clearer definition of Chinese culture is needed so that refutable implications are possible to the extent that the explanation ceases to be tautological. As for the problem that culture is itself an object for explanation, we will go one step further to explain how this culture came about in the first place as a maximizing response within a further set of constraints. Whilst the identification of institutions and rules of the game in explaining behaviour is a major contribution of institutional economists, nevertheless explanations by institutionalists are incomplete in the same sense as the cultural explanation is incomplete, because we have to go on to explain why, for a given institution, this rule and not that rule is adopted. The way to solve the problem of incomplete explanation is not to abandon the institutional explanation but to supplement it with explanations of why one institution (rule) and not another is adopted. An understanding of institutional rules contributes greatly to our understanding and prediction of human behaviour

Culture's ability to constrain behaviour in general

Culture is a concept notoriously difficult to pin down. Raymond Williams regards it as one of the two or three most complicated words in the English language (Williams, 1976/1983). There were already over several hundred definitions in 1952 (Kroeber and Kluckhohn, 1952). As pointed out by Boisot (1995):

> Culture has always been something of a portmanteau term on which scholars from diverse disciplines could each hang up their own preferred meaning . . . To devise a working definition of culture that will satisfy specialist and non-specialist alike is probably an impossible task.

In the past, sociologists tended to use a very broad definition. One famous example is that provided by Tylor (1903):

> That complex whole which includes knowledge, belief, art, law, morals, customs, and any capabilities and habits acquired by man as a member of society.

However, recognizing that such definitions are too broad to be useful, sociologists have recently adopted more narrow definitions. They seem to converge on that aspect which affects our acquisition, perception, and interpretation of information. For example: 'Culture . . . refers to the acquired knowledge that people use to interpret experience and generate social behaviour' (Spradley, 1979/1991), or 'Culture is a learned, shared, compelling, interrelated set of symbols whose meanings provide a set of orientations for members of society' (Terpstra and David, 1985).

The following is an example: 'You speak very good English,' a North American compliments a Chinese. The Chinese responds, 'Oh, no! My English still needs improving.' The North American is puzzled by the Chinese person's reply and the Chinese is unaware that he or she has violated an American cultural rule concerning how a compliment should be received (Ge et al., 1998).

Culture generally

High culture

Matthew Arnold (1822–1888) was a pre-eminent poet of the Victorian era, a lifelong educator, a pioneer in the field of literary criticism, a government official (Inspector of Schools) and an influential public figure. But one of his most enduring legacies is his extensive body of writing on the topic of culture. Arnold saw culture as what has become known as high culture – 'contact with the best which has been thought and said in the world' – as the crucial component of a healthy democratic state. Arnold's view of culture, as involving such characteristics as 'beauty,' 'intelligence,' and 'perfection,' tends to assume that these values exist in the abstract and are the same for all human societies. His argument, then, is openly political: he feels that if more people will share and pursue his notions of beauty, truth, and perfection – of culture – then the world will be a better place.

Ordinary culture

Raymond Williams was an early pioneer in the field of 'cultural studies.' According to one of his editors, Williams wrested culture 'from that privileged space of artistic production and specialist knowledge, into the lived experience of the everyday.' The following excerpt is from an essay Williams wrote in 1958, entitled 'Culture is Ordinary':

> Culture is ordinary: that is the first fact. Every human society has its own shape, its own purposes, and its own meanings. Every human society expresses these, in institutions, and in arts and learning. The making of a society is the finding of common meanings and directions, and its growth is an active debate and amendment under the pressures of experience, contact, and discovery, writing themselves into the land. The growing

society is there, yet it is also made and remade in every individual mind. The making of a mind is, first, the slow learning of shapes, purposes, and meanings, so that work, observation and communication are possible. Then, second, but equal in importance, is the testing of these in experience, the making of new observations, comparisons, and meanings. A culture has two aspects: the known meanings and directions, which its members are trained to; the new observations and meanings, which are offered and tested. These are the ordinary processes of human societies and human minds, and we see through them the nature of a culture: that it is always both traditional and creative; that it is both the most ordinary common meanings and the finest individual meanings. We use the word culture in these two senses: to mean a whole way of life – the common meanings; to mean the arts and learning – the special processes of discovery and creative effort. Some writers reserve the word for one or other of these senses; I insist on both, and on the significance of their conjunction. The questions I ask about our culture are questions about deep personal meanings. Culture is ordinary, in every society and in every mind.

(Compiled from: http://www.wsu.edu:8001/vcwsu/commons/topics /culture/culture-index.html (accessed June 2004), permission granted by Dr Richard Law, Washington State University)

Another example is given by Gombrich (1960) who juxtaposed Dürer's (1515) woodcut of a rhinoceros, Heath's (1789) engraving, *Rhinoceros of Africa* and Schulthess's (1957) photograph of an African rhinoceros. Dürer relied on second-hand descriptions for his woodcut and it was one of the first images of a rhinoceros for Europeans. Bruce, when publishing Heath's engraving, claimed that his was done from life and criticized various inaccuracies of Dürer's image. However, when one looks at the three images, one is struck by the fact that Heath's engraving bears more similarity to Dürer's image than to the photograph. As noted by Gombrich, Dürer's woodcut established the European's 'schema' of the rhinoceros and constrained the way subsequent Europeans perceived and interpreted images of a rhinoceros. As summarized by Boisot (1995): 'Various students of culture take the structuring and sharing of information as central to their definition of culture'.

This is not the place to delve too deeply into a precise definition of culture, nor is this necessary because our focus is only on Chinese culture. Suffice to say that we are concerned with the relevance of the information acquisition, perception and interpretation aspects of culture in economic explanations. Economists are concerned with cost/benefit analysis and information cost is increasingly recognized as critical to many real world phenomena. However, it is usually the quantity of information that many economists are interested in. Its qualitative aspect is often ignored.

What is meant by the quality of information is the structuring of data. There is scarcity not only of the quantity of data, but also of the structures for interpreting data. With rapid technical developments in collecting and disseminating data, such as the Internet, which has brought about the so-called information explosion, the qualitative aspect of data is becoming relatively more scarce than its quantitative aspect. Yet this is what theories are all about: economizing devices to let us screen, interpret and form opinions about data. Academics whose existence is justified by their contribution to the building and quality control of theories, underestimate the importance of the qualitative aspect of information. Culture is to others what theories are to academics. Culture both economizes and constrains information gathering and interpretation generally. Behaviour will therefore be constrained as a result. So while a precise definition of culture is not given, its general relevance is emphasized to put the subsequent discussion of Chinese culture into perspective.

Economics explains behaviour based on people's expectations. Culture determines to a large extent the formation of such expectations in both senses of the word 'expectation'; the normative sense about ethical and other cultural values and the positive informational sense of prediction about how people will react.

While placing great importance on culture for constraining behaviour in general, such constraints are not absolute. The problem with social constructionists' arguments about culture is that there is no mechanism by which culture can change. It is accepted that because of the very nature of culture, change is slow. However, given the argument that culture is itself determined by a wider set of constraints, it will change as this wider set of constraints changes.

Chinese culture defined

Turning to Chinese culture faces us with a formidable task. Unfortunately it is outside the scope of this book to pin down Chinese culture. What is needed is a proxy for Chinese culture. Confucianism is taken as the proxy. Taoism and Buddhism are the other two important philosophies or religions that have influenced Chinese culture, though their influence on the social aspect of a person is less important. However, we can still find elements in these two philosophies that might have assisted *guanxi* practice in minor ways. Many writers have taken Confucianism as forming the major part of the Chinese culture, not least because, as noted by Liang Chi-chao, it is a 'philosophy of life'.

Cheng (1972) characterized Chinese philosophy, including Confucianism, Taoism and Buddhism, in terms of its pragmatism: 'Chinese philosophy has been concerned from the very beginning with the practical question of advancing the well-being of the individual and the order and harmony of society and state.' It is interesting to note that Taoism and Confucianism emerged during the Spring and Autumn (770 BC to 476 BC) and Warring States (475 BC to 221 BC) periods when the kings of the states were eager to find an ideology that would strengthen the state and even enable it to conquer other states. The practical orientation of these ideologies or philosophies is therefore not surprising.

Confucianism

It is not possible to do justice to Confucianism in this short treatment, particularly as 'Confucianism contains many interpretations within it; it is a live set of ideas which has developed and changed over time' (Redding, 1990). Rather, most salient and non-controversial aspects will be presented with a focus on the way it has constrained behaviour in such a manner to make *guanxi* practice possible.

Chinese culture, with Confucianism at its centre, makes human beings into relational animals. A relational or network perspective pervades the Chinese worldview. Even in the concept of causation, Needham's authoritative study of the development of science in China noted that the Chinese way of approaching it is

> to systematize the universe of things and events into a structural pattern which conditioned all the mutual influences of its different parts . . . On the Greek world view, if a particle of matter occupied a particular place at a particular time, it was because another particle had pushed it there. On the [Chinese] view, the particle's behaviour was governed by the fact that it was taking its place in a 'field of force' alongside other particles that are similarly responsive: causation here is not 'responsive' but 'environmental'.
>
> (Needham, 1978)

The Chinese do not emphasize relationship in the abstract. In fact, the Chinese are noted for their lack of abstractions (Nakamura, 1964). To them the most concrete and unavoidable human relationship is the family and this is where Confucius begins. In the Chinese ethical system, the ultimate judgement about how to behave is not based on any remote religious idea conceived in abstract terms, but instead on family piety; something immediately accessible (Redding, 1990). To put it another way, Confucius seems to have found a third alternative to the difficult Hobbesian choice between the Leviathan or a ruthless state of nature, based on something with which everyone should have first-hand experience, the family. As Confucius' disciple You Zi said in the Confucian Analects, 'Filial piety and fraternal submission! – Are they not the root of all benevolent actions?' (*The Analects* I.2. quoted by Hsieh, 1967).

As only natural for one who was concerned with social order and its maintenance, when Confucius looked around for inspiration he must have been struck, as economists who adopt such a grim view of human nature would be struck, by the way the family can be organized relatively harmoniously into a very productive unit. The problem of cooperation seems to be solved without any violence. In place of selfish people who were always in conflict with each other, there was this unit, the family, within which there is sacrifice, selfless love and harmony. If only the magic behind this unit could be multiplied to the whole of society, then the whole issue of social order would be solved!

It is interesting to note that when Deng Xiaoping tried to reform China's economy in the early 1980s, the first policy that had a dramatic effect on productivity was the *Baocan daohu* – (subcontracting to the unit of the family). Deng seemed to understand that the family was the largest cooperative unit that could be mobilized without any improvements in the legal system exactly because this unit does not need the sanction of the law to ensure cooperation.

Confucius and families

Meng I Tzu asked about the meaning of filial piety. Confucius said, 'It means "not diverging (from your parents)."' Later, when Fan Chih was driving him, Confucius told Fan Chih, 'Meng Sun asked me about the meaning of filial piety, and I told him "not diverging."' Fan Chih said, 'What did you mean by that?' Confucius said, 'When your parents are alive, serve them with propriety; when they die, bury them with propriety, and then worship them with propriety.'

Meng Wu Po asked about the meaning of filial piety. Confucius said, 'The main concern of your parents is about your health.'

Tzu Lu asked about the meaning of filial piety. Confucius said, 'Nowadays filial piety means being able to feed your parents.

continued

But everyone does this for even horses and dogs. Without respect, what's the difference?'

Tzu Hsia asked about filial piety. Confucius said, 'What is important is the expression you show in your face. You should not understand "filial" to mean merely the young doing physical tasks for their parents, or giving them food and wine when it is available.'

Confucius placed great importance on the family and filial piety became a central feature of Chinese culture. Children were expected to put the interests of the family above their own aspirations. Family life was seen as a training ground for life in society as Chinese culture was preserved in the home. It is at home in the family that the child learns to deal with problems that he or she will face later in the world. The family is responsible for educating the child to be a good member of society. Confucius emphasized the importance of education, the aim of which is to turn people into good family members, responsible members of society, and good subjects of the emperor.

Therefore the stereotyped view of the Chinese family emerged as that of a large extended family, with several generations and nuclear families all living under one roof, being a self sufficient and self-help institution for its members, providing child care and the care of the elderly. But this may no longer be true to its full extent for the modern Chinese family, particularly those living in the West. However, the Chinese continue to emphasize the values of family and to maintain close family links. There is a strong bond between parents, children and other family members. It is still customary that Chinese parents expect all their children to return home for the Chinese New Year Eve dinner and other festive celebrations.

A somewhat contrary view was expressed by Chris Patten (1998):

> . . . I often heard references in Hong Kong and elsewhere in Asia to the close bonds, fierce loyalties and strong sense of duty associated with the patriarchal family, and I saw some evidence of this too. But I also often noted that the greatest beneficiary of the patriarchal family was, not surprisingly, the patriarch.
>
> (Compiled from: http://www.globaled.org/chinaproject/confucian/reading1.html, http://www.birmingham.gov.uk/GenerateContent?CONTENT_ITEM_ID=777andCONTENT_ITEM_TYPE=0andMENU_ID=10080andEXPAND=10071 (accessed June 2004))

The intention to rely on the family can be seen from the following frequently quoted sayings from *Book of Mencius*: 'Treat with reverence the elders in your own family, so that the elders in other families shall be similarly treated; treat with kindness the young in your own family, so that the young in other families shall be similarly treated' (*Book of Mencius* I.A.7). Mencius also held it to be true that 'the root of the empire is in the state, and the root of the state is in the family' (*Book of Mencius* IV.A.5 quoted by Hsieh, 1967).

The *Book of Rites* also emphasized that 'As the people are taught filial piety and brotherly love at home, with reverence toward the elder and diligent care for the aged in the community, they constitute the way of a great king; and it is along this line that states as well as families will become peaceful' (*Book of Rites* X.45 quoted by Hsieh, 1967).

In fact, the importance placed on the family by Confucians was so great that to love others instead of one's own parents would be regarded as a treacherous act (*The Classic of Filial Piety*, IX. quoted by Hsieh, 1967).

This is also evident in the Chinese emphasis on the ritual of ancestor worship. Even today, the Chinese sweep the grave of their ancestors twice a year, once on Qing Ming Festival in spring and once on Chong Yang Festival in autumn. Both are public holidays in Hong

Kong; this is two days out of an annual total of fourteen public holidays. This could be seen a great waste of resources if it was not interpreted in the light of the great gain from social order by reinforcing the value of the family.

Another example is that very often land, a precious income-generating asset in agricultural China as well as something regarded by the Chinese as having very strong emotional elements, had to be mortgaged in late imperial China when households found it necessary to raise large sums of cash for rituals such as marriages or funerals. Myers (1982) observed:

> Often a heavy burden for members of the household, these rituals nonetheless served to reinforce the neo-Confucian ethic of ancestor worship . . . Although ritual and compulsory gift-giving may not appear rational to modern eyes, these manifestations of Confucian cultural values under-girded powerful behavioral incentives which made the Chinese household a veritable economic engine of accumulation and population enhancement.

The paramount role of the family could cause problems as in the famous dilemma of a person who knows that his father has committed a crime. Should he report the father to the authorities? The answer given by Confucius is no! 'The father should conceal the son's crime and the son should conceal the father's crime. The right thing is then done' (*Analects*, XIII, 18, as quoted by Bodde, 1981).

Taking the family as the prototype of social order, the love, concern and mutual assistance between human beings, which are often displayed naturally within the family, are now transformed into the highest ideal of the Confucians and are termed *ren*. To achieve this ideal, the Confucians prescribed *li*: Yan Yuan asked about *ren*. The Master said, 'To restrain oneself and conform to *li* is *ren* . . .' (*Analects*, XII.1 as quoted by Bodde, 1981).

In fact, Confucianism has also been termed *Li Jia* (Li-ism). It is through the prescription of *li* that we can achieve a more concrete idea of the model of social order that Confucians have in mind.

For those inculcated with Chinese culture, such a view of the world (their social construction of reality) is a major factor in the formation of their expectations about how they themselves and others behave. It is therefore important to delve in more detail into some of the important contents of *li*. This requires an analysis of *Wulun*, which governs various relationships, and a description of the general guidelines defined by *li*.

In extending the nature of the relationships in the family to other relationships, a system of obligation is prescribed. Such Confucian ethics can be seen most clearly in the Confucian moral tenets concerning the *Wulun* (the five human relations) and the *San Gang* (the three bonds).

According to the *Doctrine of the Mean* XX.8; the duties of universal obligation are five, and the virtues wherewith they are practised are three. The duties are those between emperor and minister, between father and son, between husband and wife, between elder brother and younger, and those between friends. These five are the duties of universal obligation.

San Gang describes the bonds between the emperor and the minister, father and son as well as husband and wife. As prescribed by *San Gang*, the emperor should lead the minister, the father should lead the son and the husband, the wife. From this reading, it seems a rather strict hierarchical order is set. However, the situation is not that clear if we look at the virtues that govern *Wulun*, called *Wuchang* (the five virtues).

Mencius (*Book of Mencius* III.A.IV.8) specifies the nature of the virtues or duties:

> . . . between father and son, there should be affection; between sovereign and minister, righteousness; between husband and wife, attention to their separate functions; between old and young, a proper order; and between friends, trustworthiness.

The moral duties specified by *San Gang* and *Wuchang* are paramount to Confucucians. Cu Hsi, a very important Confucian scholar in the Ming dynasty, condemned Taoism and Buddhism for neglecting these duties: 'The mere fact that they discard the Three Bonds . . . and the Five Constant Virtues . . . is already a crime of the greatest magnitude. Nothing more need be said about the rest' Chan (1963).

So although the relationships under *Wulun* may be unequal as specified by *San Gang*, they are not one-sided. Reciprocity and mutual obligation are present; the superior party owes a duty to the inferior party. For example, although under filial piety (the most important relationship), the father expects loyalty and obedience from the son, he must also reciprocate by taking care of and nurturing the son. The father has inescapable duties and obligations in the relationship (Westwood, 1992). A widely quoted paragraph from the ancient text *San Zi Jing* (The Three-Character Classic) states: 'The father will be at fault if he only feeds and does not educate his offspring'. More recently Westwood (1992) states; 'The dominant party must be shown respect and obedience but at the same time offer care and protection to the subordinate party'.

Even though the emperor has nearly absolute power, in theory at least, he is understood to have duties to his subjects. If he does not treat his subjects well, then he will lose the 'Mandate from Heaven' – his legitimacy to rule. If the emperor himself has to observe the rules of relationships (Hsieh, 1967), then as noted by Westwood (1992), 'most relations are characterized by such mutual obligations'.

From this, it seems that everyone is bounded by a certain 'contract' with others, though an unequal one, as signalled by *San Gang*, and that the whole of society is connected by a nexus of contracts between individuals. No negotiations are, of course, possible for such contracts. It is as if Confucian ethics has already supplied the standard terms. Mutual obligations exist which are similar to contracts. Each person knows what is expected from them and what they can expect from others.

The general rules of relationships are prescribed by *li* and, based mainly on an analysis of the Confucian classics conducted by Li and Wu (1996), are summarized as:

Guihe (harmony)

As noted by a disciple of Confucius (and collected in the *Analects* I.14): 'Harmony defines good conduct of *li*'. Conflict is inevitable in human relationships. The prescription of harmony nonetheless forms an important principle for at least beginning to solve such conflicts.

Zhizhong (never going to extremes)

As elaborated in the Chinese Classic, the *Doctrine of the Mean*, one should never go to extremes. People should try to be balanced in their views and actions so that when there is a conflict, each side moves towards the position of the opposite number so that the gap could eventually be bridged.

Shurang (forgiving and yielding)

Confucius often advocated forgiveness and giving way as an important step in achieving harmony. Yielding has always been an important element in *li* as illustrated by an ancient saying even before the times of Confucius: 'Giving way is the main thing about *li*'.

Zhong shin (loyalty and trustworthiness)

In the *Analects*, Confucius compared a person who does not honour his words with a cart without its axles; the cart will not run and the person cannot be a proper human being. Zeng Zhi, a disciple of Confucius also claimed; 'I reflect three times a day on whether I have been disloyal towards others or whether I have not honoured my words towards my friends'.

Shenyan (cautious with words)

Confucius often judges people by how they speak. For him, the more and the better one speaks, the less likely this person is to be virtuous. He once said: 'A person who is too skilful with his words and attractive in appearance is seldom a person who can achieve *ren*'. A virtuous person is usually 'Slow in speech but quick in action.'

Zhichi (knowing shame)

'To know shame amounts to bravery'. The ability to feel shameful is extolled as a virtue. This lends support to face as an effective control on the behaviour of the Chinese because the punishment for losing face is to feel shame.

Whilst, the influence of Taoism and Buddhism on relationships has been much less than Confucianism, some elements have contributed. The Taoist ideal of *Wuwei* has discouraged government intervention into the private lives of the people, which incidentally includes the adjudication of disputes in private agreements. Also, the Taoist concept of *Yin* and *Yang* has emphasized that one should not go to extremes and discourages more calculative orientations in business. One can never win everything. The natural way is the balancing of opposing forces; co-existence, not complete annihilation of the opposition. *Tai chi,* one kind of Chinese *Wushu,* takes yielding as its main tactic.

Buddhist thought is similar to Taoism in its non-materialist orientation. Its otherworldliness means that it is not very relevant to business practice. However, the idea of *Yin* (Cause) and *Guo* (Result) in the vulgarized form of Buddhism, which is much more popular than the non-vulgarized form, does have important implications for enforcement of contracts. Outstanding accounts should always be settled and if they are not settled in this world, they will be settled after life.

The constraint of Confucian culture on *guanxi* behaviour

Confucianism has constrained Chinese behaviour in such a way as to enable *guanxi* to solve the problem of contract enforcement. Whilst not every person exposed to Chinese culture has a systematic view of Confucianism, an understanding of Confucianism does give a flavour of how immersed in personal relationships the Chinese people are. Confucianism forms at least the initial concepts, theories and stock of knowledge of an individual who will know how to behave and will have expectations about how others will behave based on such a stock of knowledge. It should not be inferred that the Chinese follow strictly such rules or that they are very trusting. There are various means by which the Chinese guard against opportunistic behaviour and these show that the Chinese are sceptical. However, the cultural climate is such that an initial expectation of good faith on both sides is possible between people who are unfamiliar with each other, and this provides the possibility for further development.

From the Confucian worldview it is impossible to live outside a network of relationships. People are defined by their relationships with others. Their worth is judged by how well they treat those related to them. The highest ideal for Confucians is *ren,* which is nothing but the compassion that one should show to others. It is not the realization of the potential that God has given us, or how well we have done God's will. Most elements of *guanxi* practice (*guanxi* base, *guanxi* reference, personalism, *guanxi* as totality of relation, and face) make use of a person's relationship network to enforce a contract. For some, a person's network provides collateral. That is, if the contract is not honoured, then not only would the defector destroy his relationship with his trading partner, but he would also damage his relationship with others in his relationship network. One important reason why this has a high opportunity cost is that within a cultural environment dominated by the Confucian ideal and worldview, a person's relationship with others accounts for most of what is valuable to this person.

If there is a problem of contract enforcement, instead of suing in court, a person could go to the relationship network and ask that those related to the defector exert influence on him to perform his duties. With emphasis on the avoidance of being shamed, one is encouraged to allow oneself to be judged by those around one. A system of mutual supervision is instituted, so cheating and going back on one's promises are thus discouraged.

In fact, Confucian cultures such as those that exist in China and Japan have been depicted by some as 'shame' cultures, as against the 'guilt' cultures of the West (Hsu, 1949, Eberhard, 1967). As noted by Benedict (1946):

> A society that inculcates absolute standards of morality and relies on men's developing a conscience is a guilt culture by definition . . . True shame cultures rely on external sanctions for good behavior, not, as true guilt cultures do, on an internalized conviction of sin. Shame is a reaction to other people's criticism.

Renqing rules are generally followed when parties initially engage in *guanxi* building and the Confucian *li* has prescribed general behaviour towards other human beings. Such *li* requirements, as ideals, are influential in the crystallization of the *renqing* rules of the people. We can see from the *li* prescriptions (harmony, never going to extremes, forgiveness, loyalty and trustworthiness, and emphasis on deeds rather than words) that one is required to think from the position of the person on the other side of the relationship. A display of such virtues also lowers the expectation of risk that the other party will refuse to honour contracts.

Specifically, an emphasis on harmony encourages arbitration and provides a strong motive for establishing mutually agreeable terms. Emphasis on loyalty, integrity and benevolence encourages contract compliance. The emphasis on deeds rather than words is particularly interesting. It seems Confucians understood very well that the problem with agreements is not just the coming to terms, but also the enforcement of such terms. To say one agrees is one thing, but to act as though one really agrees is another. So this prescription seems to relate directly to contract enforcement.

By conforming to the prescriptions of *li*, a strong signal of goodwill is displayed even before there are any transactions. The opposite side is also expected to display such gestures of goodwill. This initial display as well as the expectation of goodwill greatly facilitates the development of *guanxi*.

The importance of this initial expectation and gesture of goodwill should not be underestimated, as is evidenced in Axelrod's (1981, 1984) famous tournaments. In his study of cooperative behaviour without third party sanction, game theorists were asked to devise strategies for the computer to participate in games of the repeated Prisoner's Dilemma (PD) genre. A whole range of designs was submitted and they were placed against each other to play a repeated game of PD. It turns out that one of the most successful strategies is the 'tit-for-tat' strategy. It consistently outperformed other strategies in subsequent tournaments. In this strategy a partner/opponent will reciprocate or retaliate in exactly the same way as its partner/opponent has done to it in the last round. If the counter-party cooperates, it will cooperate in the next round. If the counter-party defects, it will defect in the next round. Now the interesting thing about this strategy is that its first move is always to cooperate. Now to take just one example: when two computers with this same strategy meets each other in the tournament, each will be able to reap the greatest joint score because as the first move is to cooperate for both, they will continue to cooperate in subsequent moves according to 'tit-for-tat'. However, if defection is assigned as the first move for the 'tit-for-tat' strategy, quite the opposite will result because the whole game will become defection against defection and both will suffer heavy losses. So the first move can be critical and an initial display as well as expectation of good-will resulting from an adherence to the Confucian prescriptions of *li* is analogous to having cooperated as the first move. Mutually beneficial *guanxi* can thus be developed.

It is interesting to note that, in fact, early Confucians had a debate among themselves on human nature. *Mencius* held that human nature is inherently good and that people become bad only after they are exposed to experience after birth. The group led by Shun Tze held that human nature is inherently bad and education after birth can improve them. Eventually, *Mencius's* proposition prevailed. This further echoes our discussion about what to expect in the first move of the prisoner's dilemma game – cooperation should be expected – because human nature is inherently good. It is, however, ironic that in Confucianism there are many prescriptions and exhortations about roles and appropriate behaviour. This seems to imply that human beings can be rather nasty, or else why are so many rules and so much advice on appropriate behaviour necessary? Or maybe it is not ironic, but expedient in making explicit the actual assumptions about human nature behind Confucian prescriptions. Though the assumption of an inherently good human nature may not be consistent in terms of logic, to do so seems quite consistent in terms of the overall cause of Confucianism in order to advocate a harmonious social order. It is hard to imagine, at least for the unsophisticated, that Confucians could say that, in fact, we are all by nature bad.

Government inculcation of Confucianism in imperial China

The way that Confucians spell out how their ideology is to be practised makes it readily accessible to the ordinary person. Its adoption was also reinforced by strong institutional arrangements that inculcated the Chinese with the Confucians' worldview.

Confucius and government

Confucian sayings:

Good government obtains when those who are near are made happy, and those who are far off are attracted.

He who exercises government by means of his virtue may be compared to the north polar star, which keeps its place and all the stars turn towards it.

If you would govern a state of a thousand chariots (a small-to-middle-size state), you must pay strict attention to business, be true to your word, be economical in expenditure and love the people.

There were two interrelated facets in the tradition founded by Confucius: government and proper social order were a major concern on the one hand, and on the other it presented a profound vision of the qualities and modes of conduct necessary to be a full and worthy human being. These were intimately linked, for in the Confucian view morality or humanity consisted primarily in the cultivation and conduct of proper social relationships and the essence of government was morality. Confucius was China's first private educator. His role was to train young men for service in government and his most fundamental conviction was that the essential preparation for such service must be character formation: true learning was moral learning, and society should be ruled (ordered) by a meritocracy based on such learning.

(Compiled from: http://faculty.washington.edu/mkalton/Neo Confucianism. htm (accessed June 2004))

Confucius was also concerned with the behaviour of rulers and officials in government. He was not interested in the political aspect of government but in the moral aspect of the men. He believed that good men must be in control of the government to solve problems that affect the people. Confucius believed and taught that the Te', the moral force within rulers, was contagious, and, if reflected by the men in government, the country would become more moral. Good government was more important to Confucius than it was to any other world religion.

Confucius wanted to show the people the way to happiness and prosperity and good moral character.

(Compiled from: http://jpdawson.com/modrelg/confuci.html (accessed June 2004))

In imperial China from the Han (206 BC to 220 AD) to the Qing dynasties (1644–1911), with the exception of the time when China was under Mongol rule (1271–1368), the major avenue by which an ordinary person could move up the social as well as the economic ladder was to become a high *renqing* official in the state's bureaucracy. The primary way to enter this bureaucracy was to go through the examination system organized by the state.

The development of the examination system in China was gradual. During Han, when the examination system was first instituted, the aristocracy still held important positions in the government. This old aristocracy's influence began to decline in Tang (618–907) when the examination system was fully developed (Fairbank *et al.*, 1973). The syllabus of the examination was nearly always limited to the Confucian classics. For example, during Ming the subject matter was limited to the Four Books, which had been selected as the essence of Confucianism in the Sung, and the Five Classics, again as interpreted by the Sung Confucian scholars of the school of Zhu Xi (Fairbank *et al.*, 1973). When the successful candidates entered officialdom, they were sent all over China to be administrators. The only training that they had received was in the Confucian Classics so it was only natural that the Confucian ideology would be the standard they would use in their official duties to judge what was right and wrong. Thus the state spread and sustained the Confucian ideology over all the empire.

But this was not the only way that Confucianism was institutionalized. The official class was relatively small compared to the population as a whole. In the early Ming period there were only 2,000 principal official posts in China's provinces. In 1800, during the Qing period, the total number of principal and minor posts was only twenty thousand. As noted by Fairbank *et al.* (1973), 'The control of the country by such a small number of mandarins . . . was feasible only because of the functions performed by the dominant elite in each locality, that is, the degree-holders or gentry'. And it is to this class that we now turn.

From the late Tang period (the twelfth century) up to the end of imperial rule many local public functions were performed by the gentry class who played a very prominent role at the local level. Individuals became gentry by securing degrees, mainly through the examination system. However, it was possible to inherit or even purchase degree status. The former method was not common, while for the latter, even if the rich did purchase degree status, they were rarely given official posts thus only admitting the rich to the gentry class but not officialdom (Fairbank *et al.*, 1973). In a society based on farming, with landowning the chief economic support for scholarly study, landlord-gentry families were very common. The peculiar strength of Confucian government lay in the many public functions that this gentry class performed. They included, for example, raising funds for and supervision of public works, building and maintaining of the local Confucian temples and ceremonies to uphold public morals, supporting schools and academies, and adjudication of civil disputes. The importance of the gentry class and its role in inculcating Confucian ideology is best summarized by Fairbank *et al.* (1973):

> The interest of the government was to maintain morale and a type of public spirit among the gentry, as opposed to selfish opportunism. To this end the Confucian temples and the Son of Heaven issued his moral exhortations . . . Thus the great tradition of learning, under the patronage of the head of the state, was used to indoctrinate the common people, while the gentry class as the local elite in turn provided leadership in the orderly life of the village.

Throughout history, the imperial government has sponsored Confucian learning. For example, the Taixue (Imperial College) was established by the government during the Han period (in 124 BC) as the highest institution of learning, and where Confucian learning dominated the curriculum (Fairbank, 1992). This institution continued through the dynasties until the end of Southern Song (1279 AD). Also, standing at the top of the Confucian intellectual pyramid under the Ming was the Hanlin Academy, a carefully selected body of outstanding metropolitan graduates who performed important literary tasks for the court. Confucian led official domination of learning continued into the Qing period (Fairbank *et al.*, 1973).

Besides the state, the family was also a strong force in the inculcation of Confucian ideology. Tales, stories and poems for children were infused with teachings of Confucian values such as filial piety, loyalty to friends and the emperor. For example, the *San Zi Jing* (The Three-Character Classic), which was the chief primer for recitation by children in Ming, Qing and the early years of the Republican government, gave in jingle form a concise summary of the basic knowledge of the Confucian doctrine in 356 alternately rhyming lines, each of three characters. Many Chinese who are now over 50 years old are still able to recite part of this primer. It is hardly surprising that parents, as head of the family, would be keen to inculcate Confucianism as filial piety is at the centre of Confucian teachings.

5 The influence of law in imperial China

Law as a practical expedience

The legal system in imperial China was most uncongenial to the ordinary person. In general, it did not present a viable alternative to private means for ensuring contract enforcement. One fundamental difference between the traditional Chinese concept of law and the legal concepts in the West is that the law in China was not regarded as an external and categorical element in society. There was no 'higher law' given to mankind through divine revelation. There was no Moses to receive golden tablets on a mountain-top from God. Instead, Confucius reasoned from daily life without the aid of any deity. He did not claim any metaphysical sanctions for his rules of propriety. For him, legal rules were but one expression of this morality – models or examples to be followed, or working rules of administration or ritual observance. Because practical expedience rather than religious principle was used to justify the law, it followed that regard for the law could be relaxed if it was in conflict with the higher principles of morality (Fairbank, 1992). An interesting point here is that China's early cosmology also shows striking points of difference from Western thought. For example, as the early Chinese had no creation myth and no creator-lawgiver out of this world, they had no first cause. As Joseph Needham (1978) pointed out, they 'assumed a philosophy of organism, an ordered harmony of wills without an ordainer'.

This clearly non-mythological and soberly sociological view of law (Bodde, 1981) is reflected in the following passage from a book written during the Han period in its explanations for the origin of law:

> Law (*fa*) has its origin in social rightness (*yi*). Social rightness has its origin in what is fitting for the many. What is fitting for the many is what accords with the minds of men. Herein is the essence of good government . . . Law is not something sent down from Heaven, nor is it something engendered by Earth. It springs from the midst of men themselves, and by being brought back [to men] it corrects itself.[1]

Also, Robson (1935) made the interesting observation that there is scarcely a country in which trial by ordeal has not been practised with the possible exception of China, where there is no hint of judgement by the gods. Trial by ordeal means that suspects are tried by forces not under human control. For example, they might be put under water for over three minutes, and those who survive are regarded as innocent as this is a signal from the gods.

In fact, for the Chinese, the law is but one of several guidelines for decisions or judgements. This is well illustrated in the common Chinese saying: *Heqing, heli, hefa.* (Have regard to the sentiments of the people involved; follow the dictates of reason; conform to the law.) The law is not divine. Moreover, in judging on the basis of the order of 'the three *hes*', conformity to the law has the lowest priority.

Although dynasties succeeding the Qin dynasty adopted Confucianism as the only officially sanctioned ideology, leading to a 'confucianization' of the law, the Qin dynasty's legalistic code retained its influence in subsequent dynasties. This legalist influence manifested itself in the penal nature of the imperial codes and the absence of civil law. These features are traceable to the legalist concept of law as an instrument of control by the state. Despite their name, legalists are not advocating the 'rule of law', but rather 'rule by law'.[2]

It is generally agreed among scholars that Chinese law is penal in nature.[3] As noted by Chen (1973):

[The law] was for the most part penal in nature, matters of civil law being left to custom and usage and mainly to private arbitration . . . The emphasis on penal code in Chinese law meant that matters of a civil nature were either ignored entirely or were given only limited treatment under criminal law . . . The law played only a secondary role in defending the individual rights – especially the economic rights, and not at all in defending such rights against the government or the state. The only purpose of the law was to prevent and to deter the commission of criminal acts.[4]

Legalism

Legalism is a political philosophy that does not address higher questions pertaining to the nature and purpose of existence. It is concerned with the most effective way of governing society. The legalist tradition derives from the principle that the best way to control human behaviour is through written law rather than through ritual, custom or ethics. The two principal sources of legalist doctrine were the Book of Lord Shang and the Han Fei-tzu. The Book of Lord Shang teaches that laws are designed to protect the stability of the state from the people, who are innately selfish and ignorant. There is no such thing as objective goodness or virtue; it is obedience that is of paramount importance.

The Han Fei-tzu advocates a system of laws that enable the ruler to govern efficiently and even ruthlessly. Text books, apart from law books, are useless and rival philosophies such as Confucianism are dismissed as 'vermin'. The ruler is to conduct himself with great shrewdness, keeping his ministers and family at a distance and not revealing his intentions. Strong penalties should deter people from committing crime. Laws should reward those who obey them and punish severely those who dare to break them, even if the result of this would on the face of it appear to be undesirable. As an example from Han Fei-tzu, if a gate guard goes to fetch a blanket for the king who has just dozed off,

continued

he is being irresponsible to his official duty and deserves punishment. Thus it is guaranteed that every action taken is predictable. In addition, the system of law ran the state, not the ruler. If the law is successfully enforced, even a weak ruler will be strong.

The origins of legalist thought are unclear. It was, however, Han Fei-tzu (d. 233 BC) who systematized the various strands of legalism in his work the Han Fei-tzu. Han Fei-tzu had been taught by the Confucianist, Hsun-tzu, whose philosophy claimed that people were basically evil but could be guided towards goodness (as opposed to the alternative more benevolent Confucian movement). Han Fei-tzu adopted and developed Hsun-tzu's negative pessimistic attitude towards human nature by teaching that people were so bad that they needed to be controlled by strong government and strict laws. This principle was put into practice by the Qin dynasty, which on unifying China in 221 BC, destroyed the feudal system and placed the country under a single monarch. Under the Qin dynasty land was privatized, a uniform law code was established, and weights, measures and currency were standardized. Confucianism was severely persecuted; hundreds of Confucian scholars were killed and virtually all Confucian texts were destroyed.

Legalism achieved what all the other philosophies strove for – unification of China. The Qin dynasty, operating under the legalist philosophy, finally unified China in 221 BC. In this light, legalism was a success. However, the Qin dynasty was dissolved only 14 years after its founding. The Qin emperor was ruthless in his use of legalism, punishing even small crimes with decapitation or the loss of a hand or foot. Books and scholars that held beliefs against legalism (such as Confucianism) were destroyed. The people were heavily taxed and forced into labour on major government projects. The Qin emperor successfully put the fear and respect of the law and government into the people, but it was too much. After his death, a combination of plotting ministers and peasant rebellions caused the end of legalism as the ruling philosophy of China.

The harshness of the legalist Qin was remembered and in response the following dynasty, the Han, distanced itself from legalism and made its main rival, Confucianism, the official philosophy. So although much of legalism seems to make good sense (such as equality under the law, and government according to merit), memories of the abuse of the law under the Qin has kept legalism in a bad light throughout Chinese history.

In Christianity as well as in other religions in their fundamentalist form, legalism is still extant today. In Christianity it remains the literal adherence to the law, interpreted as following a strict and literal interpretation of the Bible.

(Compiled from: http://www.geocities.com/tokyo/springs/6339/Legalism.html, http://www.nationmaster.com/encyclopedia/Legalism-(philosophy) (accessed June 2004))

Both the words *fa* and *xing*, which are used sometimes together, sometimes interchangeably, to denote the law, carry the meaning of punishment. The original meaning of the word *xing* was punishment. The Chinese character for *xing* contains a symbol that means knife. This has prompted Bodde (1981) to note that there is every reason to believe that such punishments as nose-cutting, leg-cutting, castration and the like were current in China well before the enactment of any systems of written law. Later it was extended to also mean the written prohibitions whose violation would result in punishments (Bodde, 1981). *Xing* frequently occurred in early legal writing both alone, in combination with *fa* (as in *xingfa*), or as an alternative for *fa*. As noted by Bodde (1981): 'Until as recently as the administrative reforms of 1906, this idea [of the nature of the law] was perpetuated in the name of the highest governmental legal organ, the *Xing Bu* or Ministry of Punishment'. On the other hand, the word *fa* moved from meaning the law to also include the meaning of punishment: 'So closely is *fa* associated with punishment, that the word has become a synonym of the word punishment' (Schwartz, 1957). In fact, in the old days, the cane used by parents to punish disobedient children was called *jia fa* (family *fa*).

Demonstrating that, for legalists, the law is a means of state control and not an end in itself, Schwartz (1957) has noted that the term *fazi* (law-rule), when introduced in China in the early twentieth century, was often taken to mean the inculcation of discipline in the undisciplined Chinese masses. In other words, it was understood as a rule by law and not the rule of law.

The oppressive nature of the imperial codes, even after Confucianism was embraced by the state, is revealed in the near absolute power of the emperor who can kill as he pleases with a minimum of legal procedures:

> [T]he emperor's role [is] a source of spontaneous, irrational, or unpredictable acts . . . [T]he emperor was considered to have an arbitrary and unbridled power of life and death . . . [M]ost striking is the almost universal acceptance of the emperor's decision to execute an official. There is no court of appeal . . . This leads one to wonder whether western and modern Chinese scholars have underestimated the transcendental role of the emperor in the Chinese belief system.
>
> (Fairbank, 1992)

It is therefore little wonder that civil law never developed in imperial China. With such a legalist orientation of the law, people found the court of law best avoided, rather than used. A common Chinese saying reflects this: 'While alive, the court is to be avoided. After death, hell is to be avoided'.

Confucian and legalist orientation of the law

Legal thought in China has often been portrayed as a struggle between the legalist and Confucian schools. There are marked differences relating to law between the two schools as illustrated by the following passages:

> Confucius: If you lead the people by political measures and regulate them by penal laws, they will merely avoid

transgressing them but will have no sense of honour. If you lead them by the practice of virtue and regulate them by the inculcation of good manners, they will not only keep their sense of honour but will also be thoroughly transformed.

(*Analects* II.3, from Wu, 1967)

Shang Yang (legalist school – d.338 BC): If you govern by penal laws, the people will fear; being fearful, they will commit no villainies; there being no villainies, they will find peace and happiness. If, on the other hand, you govern by mere righteousness, they will be lax; and, if they are lax, there will be disorder and the people will suffer great miseries.

(*Book of Lord Shang* VII, from Wu, 1967)

Prescriptions by the legalist school were embraced by the Qin empire, which subsequently united the whole of China under one single administrative rule. Qin's rule was however short-lived and revolts over the whole empire brought its downfall in 207 BC after 14 year in power. Han Wu Di, the second emperor of Han (the dynasty following Qin), adopted Confucianism as the officially sanctioned philosophy and suppressed all other schools of thought. Confucianism continued to receive official sanction in all subsequent dynasties with the exception of the Yuan (1271–1368).[5] Despite the Confucian dislike for law, the imperial codes continued to be adopted and developed. The strength of the imperial codes is illustrated by Fairbank (1992):

By pre-modern standards the Chinese legal codes were monuments of their kind. The great Tang code of the eighth century and its successors in the Song, Yuan, Ming, and Qiang periods still invite analysis . . . The great Qing code listed 436 main statutes and about 1,900 supplementary or sub-statutes, which provided specific penalties for specific crimes.

This continued development of the imperial codes indicates that the Chinese emperors did not really abandon legalist prescriptions. However, Chu Tung Tzu (1957) characterized the development as a 'Confucianization' of law.

Such a characterization was widely adopted by subsequent scholars.[6] Recently Hau (1997) dissented from this view, claiming that a more proper characterization should be 'legalistization of Confucianism'. Such a debate is probably more semantic than real. *Li* was present, though it occupies a much smaller role in legalist teaching, and Confucians are not advocating a total abolition of law. The legalist spirit was present all along in the imperial codes as evident in later discussion of the penal nature of such codes as well as the absolute power held by the emperor. However, the shift from a wholesale legalist orientation in Qin towards the predominantly Confucian ideology in subsequent dynasties was clear.

True to the practical orientation of all Chinese philosophy, the concern for social order is high on the priority list of Confucians. However, to serve this purpose, *li* is the more favoured instrument. Schwartz (1957) summarized the Confucian idea about social order and litigation in this way:

> *Li* is an instrument for training character, and nourishing moral force. In a society where *li* prevails, unbridled self-interest is placed under effective control from within, as it were . . . [I]n a society where men are governed by *li*, conflicts of interest can be easily resolved. Both sides will be ready to make concessions, to yield *(rang)*, and the necessity for litigation will be avoided.

If fact, to be involved in litigation (plaintiff as well as defendant) is often regarded as a disgrace as described by Fei (1943/1992):

> A system of control based on rituals *(li)* means adherence to traditional rules . . . all the actors in this society are familiar with the rules . . . Their long education since childhood has turned these exterior rules into interior habits . . . [A]ny litigation is shameful, because it indicates a lack of proper education . . . [T]he people who file cases in the courts are the same people recognized in the countryside as being morally bankrupt.[7]

The Confucian ideas about the law and litigation are reflected in many aspects of the law as well as in the orientation of magistrates. MacCormack (1996) noted that the Confucian stamp on the law included the complex penal rules that were designed to regulate in detail various family relationships. For example; the virtues of *ren,* which underlay the important set of rules that conferred privileges on the old, the young, and the mentally or physically handicapped; the rules that provided mitigation of punishment, which were identified occasionally in the commentaries as examples of the highest degree of *ren.* By contrast, the treatment of property and commerce was sparse, and the little treatment that was given could be interpreted merely as the Confucian concern for *yang min* ('nourishing the people') (Hau, 1997).

Confucianization of the law was also to be found in the people who applied it in judgements; the government officials. In addition to the state using an examination system to select government officials based solely on Confucian classics, Confucian moral standards were also a major criterion that determined their promotion or demotion, (Hau, 1997). The Confucian orientation of these officials must doubtless have been a predominant influence on how they interpreted and used the law. This was supported by the study of actual cases by Hau (1997) who confirmed that magistrates tended not to rely solely on the letter of the law to pass judgements but that Confucian values intervened to important extents. Criteria for making judgements were thus rather uncertain. Hau also found that there was a tendency to advocate compromise and discourage litigation. This dislike of litigation by Confucians is clearly indicated in the *Analects*: 'In hearing cases I am as good as anyone else, but what is really needed is to bring about that there are no cases!' (*Analects* XII.13).

For Confucians, ultimately the law was a means to be used in the ceaseless struggle to sustain a moral order (Fairbank, 1992) rather than for adjudicating on mundane matters relating to private business. What was of primary concern was the moral order.

Officials' lack of resources and incentive

The resources devoted to the practical enforcement of the law were clearly inadequate. The law was enforced by county magistrates but the yamen, their supporting offices, were understaffed and under-funded. To make matters worse, magistrates were burdened with all sorts of other duties:

> The typical county magistrate had charge of an area of three hundred square miles and a population of a quarter of a million people. A minor official in the government, [he was] faced with a large administrative task . . . The local magistrate was aided by his private secretaries or advisers and by personal servants whom he brought with him and paid himself. With their help he had to deal with the local yamen staff of semi-permanent government clerks and various underlings – runners, jailers, police, and miscellaneous attendants. The magistrate was caught up in a web of responsibility for all that occurred within his area. His jurisdiction was territorial and complete rather than functional and specialized.
>
> (Fairbank *et al.*, 1973)

The lack of funds for the yamen as well as the low pay of the officials also encouraged rampant corruption. This must have seriously undermined the credibility of the court as an independent third party in enforcing contracts and adjudicating business disputes. There was also little incentive for the officials to rigorously enforce the law, let alone private contracts:

> [H]e was to blame or praise . . . for all that took place within his jurisdiction . . . Looking forward to transfer to a new post within three years, local officials were more interested in avoiding immediate embarrassment within their areas than in fostering their long-term development . . . The result was a deeply ingrained tendency to compromise, to harmonize the elements of the local scene, not to change them.
>
> (Fairbank *et al.*, 1973)

A similar view of the Chinese officials was shared by Perdue (1987):

> The basic aim of local officials was not to control every transaction or to collect the very small extra tax income from contracts, but to save themselves the trouble of hearing lawsuits.

This was in part due to the fact that the officials were evaluated by the backlog of cases. So the fewer cases there were, the less the backlog and the better the result of the 'performance review'. Is there not a loud echo of such practices in present day administration in many countries?

The problem of the courts

As referred to earlier, in China the distance between the ruler and his subjects is characterized by the saying 'Heaven is high and the emperor is far away', to express the idea that the state and its representatives (the local magistrates whose courts epitomized the power of the state) are best avoided (Fei, 1943/1992).

Besides the Confucian ideological objection to resorting to the court and the uncongenial legalist orientation of the law, the high cost as well as the unpredictable value of litigation and other risks also reduced the willingness of the Chinese to resort to the court to resolve conflicts. In the magistrate's court, plaintiffs as well as defendants could be interrogated with prescribed forms of torture and everyone would have to pay fees to yamen underlings (Fairbank, 1992).

A respectable legal profession that was able to make litigation more accessible and predictable was not in place, although there were litigation brokers called *songshi* (litigation masters) or *songgun* (litigation tricksters) who helped people to litigate. However, they were often despised (as indicated by the rather derogative term *songgun*) and had no social status in [Chinese] society (Fei, 1943/1992). Government officials, who were evaluated by the backlog of cases, blamed them for the increases in the litigiousness of the Chinese populace and the mounting burden on the court (Macauley, 1994).

So the common view of the public that the court was not generally a viable avenue for economic redress is understandable, particularly when the court was looked upon as '[operating] vertically, from the state upon the individual, more than it did horizontally, to resolve conflicts between one individual and another' (Chen, 1973).

There were times throughout China's history when the government implied that it was willing to adjudicate on contract disputes. However, it seems that the value of using the sanctions of the court was not perceived to be high enough to justify the cost. For example, in Tang, a system of 'red documents' arose in which middlemen to land sales would affix a red seal to contract documents to indicate compliance with administrative requirements and collection of applicable taxes (Wei *et al.*, 1973; Scogin, 1994). However, such contract tax was frequently evaded and so the contracts did not receive the sanction of the court (Hansen, 1995). As noted by Perdue (1987):

> After the eleventh century, the state's contract tax rose gradually up to 20 percent of the land value. The rise in the contract tax meant the proliferation of 'white contracts,' or privately drawn-up contracts lacking an official seal . . . [L]andowners were clearly willing to put their trust in the white contracts. The lower cost of the white contracts compensated for their lesser security. It seems that the people and the state were not able to reach a price for the state's provision of a service for the legal enforcement of contracts.

An important issue discouraging the use of law as a third party to enforce private contracts in traditional China was that the law was not perceived to be independent. Independence, in the eyes of those who seek adjudication for their private contracts, must be understood to mean that the adjudicator should take the original rights and obligations as specified in the contracts as the primary or even sole criterion in making judgements. As seen, the tendency for officials to take Confucian ethics as the fundamental constraint on their judgements seriously undermined their independence. Corruption caused by under-funding of the yamen was another factor that further lowered the government's perceived credibility. It is ironic that if the official is corrupt, then he cannot be trusted, whilst if he is incorruptible, then he is probably a fervent Confucian, and thus is also not to be trusted to respect the original letter of the contract! In fact, the harm done by incorruptible officials (called *qing guan*) has been highlighted in *Lao Can You Ji* (Travel tales of Lao Can), a famous novel set in the Qing dynasty. The author took the view that the self-righteousness of incorruptible officials did more harm than corrupt officials. It seems to have been a no-win situation! Compounding this situation, the penal and administrative nature of the codes also caused a perception of the law as a means of state oppression rather than a system where justice was to be sought.

So Confucianism with its dislike of the law and litigation dominated the legal system in China. Nevertheless the legalist influence was still seen in the penal nature of the codes. Both ideologies had disincentives for the common people to appeal to the courts regarding conflicts of a business nature. Besides ideology, there was also the lack of development of civil law and local magistrate's resources to deal with conflicts regarded as private in nature. For the general public, the state was something to be feared. The high cost of litigation and lack of independence meant that it was seldom the preferred alternative for enforcing agreements. The Chinese have always treasured non-intervention by the state as in the common saying: 'Heaven is high and the emperor is far away'. A more poetic way of putting it is: 'As the sun rises I get up. As the sun sets I go to rest. I dig a well for my drink. I till the fields for my food. What has the power of the emperor to do with me?' (The ancient *Chi-jang kou* (Song of Mud Balls) in Shen Te-chien, *Ku-shih yuan* (Origins of Ancient Poetry, an Anthology of Old Poems) from Wu 1967).

6 The rationality of the traditional Chinese legal and cultural systems

An examination of the legal and cultural context in imperial China within which *guanxi* first developed has shown that, put simply, the weakness of the legal system in providing a trusted third party adjudication and enforcement of private agreements coupled with the strong relationship orientation of Chinese culture made *guanxi* a relatively efficient means of lowering the transaction cost of contract enforcement. But this analysis begs the question 'Why was the legal system not improved and why was the Confucianist ideology not replaced by another ideology that would be more conducive to economic development – just like the systems that seem to work well in the developed West today?' They seem to function at a lower transaction cost than the reliance on *guanxi*. In view of the fact that the cultural environment, especially Confucianism, has been blamed by many historians for China's backwardness and as a choice-theoretic approach is adopted here, which means that any backwardness is a result of choice, it is important that an attempt be made to at least begin to unravel this puzzle.

So if a choice-theoretic approach is justified, it must be shown that the social arrangements of traditional Chinese culture and law are themselves efficient. Here we are dealing with an extremely complicated question and will make no more than a first attempt to explain why such a seemingly inefficient arrangement is maximizing after all. The surprising stability of the Chinese system, which changed very little over a period of 2,000 years, makes it especially difficult to argue that the system was inefficient, particularly when taken together with the apparent reason for its breakdown being external and unexpected.

What is needed is an explanation of how the state formulated the system of property rights. A system of property rights is understood to be the underlying rule of the game within a state, including not just the legal system, but also norms, customs and culture; what North (1990) called informal constraints with special reference to their historical development. Few economists, with the exception of Douglass North, have done extensive work in this area and the theoretical arguments in this section are based on a modification of North's ideas, especially those presented in his 1973 book, *The Rise of the Western World* (with Thomas), and his 1981 book, *Structure and Change in Economic History*.

The question is 'Why did a system of property rights that was less costly than the one adopted by China's imperial past (such as the one adopted by the developed West at present) not evolve?'

One would not normally turn to the constituents (the ruled) for institutional innovation because the public good nature of the property rights system means that there are huge transaction costs in the form of the free rider problem for the constituents to organize the provision of such a service on their own. However, it is a different story for the ruler who could enjoy a comparative advantage in providing such a service. Given the large size of the population and area of China, there are more people to share the fixed cost of the public good. So, it seems to be more cost-effective for the Chinese ruler to provide it.

Property rights

by Armen A. Alchian

One of the most fundamental requirements of a capitalist economic system – and one of the most misunderstood concepts – is a strong system of property rights. For decades social critics

continued

in the United States and throughout the Western world have complained that 'property' rights too often take precedence over 'human' rights, with the result that people are treated unequally and have unequal opportunities. Inequality exists in any society. But the purported conflict between property rights and human rights is a mirage – property rights are human rights.

The definition, allocation, and protection of property rights is one of the most complex and difficult set of issues that any society has to resolve, but it is one that must be resolved in some fashion. For the most part social critics of 'property' rights do not want to abolish those rights. Rather, they want to transfer them from private ownership to government ownership. Some transfers to public ownership (or control, which is similar) make an economy more effective. Others make it less effective. The worst outcome by far occurs when property rights really are abolished.

A property right is the exclusive authority to determine how a resource is used, whether that resource is owned by government or by individuals. Society approves the uses selected by the holder of the property right with governmental administered force and with social ostracism. If the resource is owned by the government, the agent who determines its use has to operate under a set of rules determined, in the United States by Congress, or by executive agencies it has charged with that role.

Private property rights have two other attributes in addition to determining the use of a resource. One is the exclusive right to the services of the resource. Thus, for example, the owner of an apartment with complete property rights to the apartment has the right to determine whether to rent it out and, if so, which tenant to rent to; to live in it himself; or to use it in any other peaceful way. That is the right to determine the use. If the owner rents out the apartment, he also has the right to all the rental income from the property. That is the right to the services of the resources (the rent).

Under a private property system the market values of property reflect the preferences and demands of the rest of society. No matter who the owner is, the use of the resource is influenced by what the rest of the public thinks is the most valuable use. The reason is that an owner who chooses some other use must forsake that highest-valued use – and the price that others would pay him for the resource or for the use of it. This creates an interesting paradox: although property is called 'private,' private decisions are based on public, or social, evaluation.

The fundamental purpose of property rights, and their fundamental accomplishment, is that they eliminate destructive competition for control of economic resources. Well-defined and well-protected property rights replace competition by violence with competition by peaceful means.

(Permission to reprint Alchian, Armen A., 'Property Rights', *The Concise Encyclopedia of Economics. Liberty Fund*, Inc., ed. David R. Henderson. Library of Economics and Liberty, http://www.econlib.org/library/Enc/PropertyRights.html granted by David R. Henderson, copyright owner (accessed June 2004))

Free rider problem

In the analyses of economics and political science, free riders are actors who take more than their fair share of the benefits or do not shoulder their fair share of the costs of their use of a resource, involvement in a project, etc. The free rider problem is the question of how to prevent free riding from taking place, or at least limit its effects.

Because the notion of 'fairness' is highly subjective, free riding is usually only considered to be an economic 'problem' when it leads to the non-production or under-production of a public good, and thus to Pareto inefficiency, or when it leads to the excessive use of a common property resource.

continued

The usual example of a free rider problem is National Defense; no person can be excluded from being defended by a nation's military and thus free riders may develop who refuse or avoid paying for being defended, but are still as well guarded as everyone else in the nation. Therefore, it is usual for the government to avoid relying on volunteer donations, using *taxes* and/or conscription instead.

The problem is particularly important and troublesome when considering goods or resources to which access cannot be excluded.

(Compiled from: http://en.wikipedia.org/wiki/Free_rider_problem (accessed June 2004))

It is therefore a puzzle why a more efficient system was not developed by the state. Paradoxically, the system basically benefits the constituents but the free rider problem works against them providing it rather than the ruler. But, on the face of it, the ruler has no incentive to improve the system either even though it may be cost effective for the ruler to provide it. However, the possibility of a bargain between the ruler and the ruled means that if a more efficient system can bring great benefit to the ruled they will 'bribe' the ruler to provide it.[1]

Invariably, we turn to the behaviour of transaction costs to explain why such a trade has not occurred in China, or to be more accurate, why such a trade has not occurred to a greater extent, as would be expected. It is inaccurate to say that no such trade has occurred because the rulers did provide some public goods, protection and some form of social order and did extract payment for them, mainly by way of tax and granting of monopolies. But why did more such trade not occur?

The constraints of transaction costs on the emperors' ruling style

Basically, being the Son of Heaven, emperors could (and many did) regard the world as their apple but, due to the problem of transaction costs, it mysteriously shrunk as they tried to have a bigger bite. To rule China, an emperor had to rely on agents. This reliance was especially acute because of the sheer size of the population and area of the country. Monitoring costs could be immense and could constrain, in an important way, a ruler's method of ruling the people. Since the 'free rider problem' associated with the agents was less severe than that associated with the population as a whole, relying on agents was advantageous but could mean that 'revolutions will be palace revolutions undertaken by the ruler's agents or by a competing ruler or small elite Leninist-type groups' (North, 1981). So monitoring the agents was extremely important in the ruler's considerations.

One way to reduce the cost of monitoring is to have a smaller number of agents and it seems that Chinese emperors opted for this solution. As noted earlier, the number of government officials relative to the population was very small. Principal posts in all provinces totalled only 2,000 in the early Ming period. In 1800 (Qing dynasty) all civil officials, including minor incumbents, totalled only 20,000. The result was a class of agents of the state that was overburdened with all sorts of major and minor tasks. If the state was to increase further the workload of the officials by instituting property right changes then a much larger group of agents would be required or the changes would be unsuccessful. The failure by the government to provide official recognition of land sales contracts (red sealed) and the financing of this government service by collecting a contract tax is a case in point. The emperors seem to have opted to forsake the potential revenue gain that accompanies institutional innovations to avoid increasing the state bureaucracy, which they feared might get out of hand. They chose therefore to rely more on Confucianism as state ideology for social order and less on strict and formal control by a complicated set of legal codes.

Another important issue regarding the agency problem was recruitment. The examination system adopted by the dynasties since the Han period proved an extremely successful system for facilitating control of the agents by the emperor and securing the needed talent, as well as loyalty, for carrying out his wishes. Here again, the Confucian ideology played a very significant role:

> Confucian ideology lay at the basis of Chinese education, the ruling class was thoroughly imbued with ethical principles, concepts of loyalty to existing authority, and a strong sense of the value of rituals and decorum. Men of intellectual ability, singularly favoured as they were by the system, became the strongest supporters of the government, instead of its critics, as has happened in so many other societies. The system even won the support of the lower classes for the established order, because there was always the possibility that a man of humble birth might pass the *chin-shih* examination and eventually become one of the emperor's chief ministers.
>
> (Fairbank *et al.*, 1973)

This method of recruitment relieved the emperor of the need for the alternative method of relying on hereditary aristocrats as agents, a group which would have been much more difficult to control. So, with the appearance of the fully developed examination system in the Tang, the decline of aristocratic society commenced (Fairbank *et al.*, 1973).

If institutional innovation is carried to such an extreme that the state is trusted to pass judgment on private contracts, then an independent judiciary or something that is nearly as independent has to be established. Such a body was unthinkable for the Chinese emperors who had control high on their priority list. There was simply not enough incentive for the emperor to give up his ultimate power to adjudicate in order to share in the gain from expansion in wealth as a result of forming such a body. Their power was worth a huge sum to the emperors who were not desperate for money.

Evidence to support the paramount concern of the Chinese emperors for control is plentiful. One example is the large group of eunuchs that served in the emperors' household. Their castration effectively cut all their private links (biological as well as metaphorical) so, though they were usually of lower calibre than officials selected through the examination system, they were trusted more. One function that they served was to spy on officials to check their loyalty.

Judicial independence

An extract from the address 'Convergence and the Judicial Role: Recent Developments in China' by The Hon J. J. Spigelman AC, Chief Justice of New South Wales to the China Education Centre, University of Sydney, 11 July 2002:

> In China, the relationship between the Party and the courts remains a critical issue. The prior tradition permitted party intervention in the judicial process by the examination and approval of individual cases by party cadres, a system referred to as *shuji pian*.

> One of the first clear indications of the reform process was the instruction by the Central Committee of the Party in September 1979 abolishing this system.

> However, the Constitution adopted in 1982 reflects the continued tension.

> On the one hand, the Preamble to the Constitution refers more than once to 'the leadership of the communist party' and Article 3 states:

>> All administrative, judicial and procuratorial organs of the state are created by the people's congresses to which they are responsible and by which they are supervised.

> On the other hand, Article 5 provides:

>> All state organs, the armed forces, all political parties and public organisations and all enterprises and institutions must

---

continued

abide by the Constitution and the law. All acts in violation of the Constitution and the law must be investigated.

No organisation or individual is privileged to be beyond the Constitution or of the law.

At the level of rhetoric, something not dissimilar to a Western conception of judicial independence has emerged over the last two decades. At the very least, direct intervention by the Party in the adjudication process is no longer regarded as legitimate.

The steps that have been taken to strengthen the Chinese judiciary as a separate institution are such as to suggest that real change is intended. The independence of the judiciary from other functions of government is not a matter capable of description with absolute precision. There are questions of degree involved.

The difficulty in the case of China is the reconciliation of an independent judiciary with the maintenance of an official ideology which appears inconsistent with any level of independence.

The state is still said to be founded on the Four Cardinal Principles, namely adherence to the socialist road, the people's democratic dictatorship, Marxism-Leninism and Mao Zedong's thought (with the recent addition of Deng Xiaoping Theory) and the leading role of the Communist Party of China.

Nevertheless, some degree of institutional differentiation has appeared, even if it does not constitute a strict separation of powers. The process will obviously take time. This is not unprecedented.

English legal history is, in large measure, derived from an analogous unified concept of the state, encompassed in the idea of the Crown. In English history, the Crown also played a 'leading role'. It took centuries for the Crown to be clearly divided into its three manifestations.

First, as the embodiment of justice in the legal system; secondly, as the executive, and thirdly, as one component part of the legislature. I am not suggesting that the Secretary-General of the Communist Party of China is on the way to becoming some kind of constitutional monarch.

I am simply noting that substantial institutional differentiation is possible within a unifying concept. We could not expect that what took centuries to achieve in England, would be done within two decades in China.

The tradition of judicial independence with which we are familiar in Australia extends beyond independence from external interference to encompass independence from other judges. This is alien to Chinese practice in which a panel of judges in a particular case is expected to consult within the court.

Many cases are, in substance, decided by the court leadership rather than the panel. Steps have been taken to limit this practice but this appears to be driven more by economy and efficiency than by any principle of independence. In our tradition, the personal independence of the individual judge is recognition of professional autonomy.

A tradition of judicial independence depends on the background, quality, training and cast of mind of the judges and on their sense of collegiality. Just over two decades ago, China had no institutionalized judiciary and no judges. It now has something of the order of 30,000 superior judges and 180,000 lower court judges. Inevitably, a very substantial proportion of those who have been appointed have not had appropriate training or background. As I understand the position, a majority are retired officers of the People's Liberation Army.

continued

> In 1982, the then recently re-established Ministry of Justice, announced that 57,000 'outstanding army officers' were being assigned to the court system. The ingrained mode of decision-making of such recruits was not instinctively such as we would call 'judicial'. In recent years, determined efforts have been made to change the quality of the judiciary in terms of qualifications, competence, cast of mind and collegiality.
>
> (Permission granted by the Hon J.J. Spigelman)

The monopolistic position of the Chinese imperial state

A further important consideration for the emperors was competitors, both inside and outside the state. They determined the extent to which rulers enjoyed a secure monopoly status in providing the services of protection, design and enforcement of systems of property rights, etc. Competitors outside the state were the neighbouring states that would either try to conquer a ruler's state or attract constituents away. Competitors inside the state were those who had the military might and/or a perceived legitimate claim to rule. Competitors presented great dangers to rulers and formed an important constraint on their behaviour. An example given by North (1981) is that the institutions favouring a more efficient property rights structure and economic development were introduced during the sixteenth and seventeenth centuries in England precisely because the king needed the support of the subjects in his struggle with competitors within as well as outside the state.

So what was the position of China's rulers in terms of competitors inside and outside the state? Inside China, the institution of the examination system for recruiting agents for the ruler meant a continuous decline in the hereditary aristocracy. This eliminated a good part of the potential threat within the state. The great respect for a ruler, as if he is the father, within the Confucian ideology offered yet further support to the ruler.

As for competitors outside the state, China was in a powerful position because, unlike Europe, it had enjoyed monopoly power for the most part throughout its history. The demand for funds to pay for expensive campaigns was much less urgent than for the European states. Military technology at the time depended less on capital than on the number of men but, of course, funds could be needed for the emperor's other material pursuits. However, institutional innovation was especially risky for a ruler. Preservation of a grip on power was much more important to a ruler than incremental economic benefits. The marginal value of additional innovation could not compensate for an increase in the risk of losing control.

Fairbank (1992) characterized the difference thus:

> Modern Europe . . . at one time had emperors of France, Russia, Austria-Hungary, Germany, and the British Empire plus the Pope in Rome all making history simultaneously. China ideally, and most of the time in fact, had only one emperor on earth, like one sun in the sky . . . No European rulers governed self-sufficient lands or held the final word on law and justice, moral thought, religion, art, the military, and public works that was claimed by and for China's Sons of Heaven.

It is interesting to note that in various studies of companies of differing market power, monopolies were found to have the least incentive for innovation although they often buy innovative concepts or product designs from smaller competitors, not always with a plan to produce the new product itself but just to prevent the new product from appearing on the market. IBM failed to take the offer by Bill Gates to sell his Disk Operating System (DOS) when the latter was still managing a fledgling company and committed one of the most famous and serious mistakes in the history of business.

For European states, pressure for institutional innovations was much greater in order to increase their revenue and thus their military might as well as to compete against internal rivals. All producers face competition but, in the case of monopolies, the competition is more about gaining control of the monopoly rights itself, and thus capturing the monopoly rent and sometimes reducing the size of the rent as a result. Whereas in markets with more producers, improvement of the quality of services provided carries greater weight.

With the monopolistic power of the Chinese emperors, the concern was for protecting their monopoly rights within the state through control of their agents. The competitive game was not about improving the service of the state. For most of China's history, the weak internal competitors did not pose an important threat to the ruler's monopoly power so there was little need for the emperor to sell his rights in order to raise funds for military campaigns.

The efficiency of the traditional system

It can be seen that the present day Western style system of property rights was not the preferred way of governing for the Chinese emperors. The monopoly nature of the Chinese state in terms of weak internal and external competitors (until the nineteenth century) and the transaction costs in allowing a sharing in the fruits of economic growth through institutional innovations made the sale of the emperor's rights for gain unattractive. On the other hand, the Confucian-Legalist amalgam served his interests much better.

In fact, North (1981) might well be talking about China when he noted:

> Stagnant states can survive as long as there is no change in the opportunity cost of the constituents at home or in the relative strength of competitor states. This last condition usually implies that the state approaches the status of a monopoly and is surrounded by weak states (and there are no net gains to a ruler in acquiring these states).

An interesting point about the system of control adopted by the Chinese emperors is that even the constituents, that is, those on the other side of the equation, found it acceptable too. This is important because otherwise the whole scheme would be self-defeating as the cost of governing would increase and a much larger group of agents would be required. The constituents are happy because such a system means that they are more immune from the arbitrary power of the state. The examination system also means that there is a possible channel for even the poorest to be upwardly mobile. The possibility of winning in the game means a higher opportunity cost for overthrowing it.

The information cost of the consequences of institutional innovations is extremely high, so for rulers and subjects to draw lessons from history is rational. In this regard; the history of the Warring States and Qin dynasty must have weighed heavily on all subsequent rulers. The breaking up of Chou into Warring States (which were once agents of Chou) is a clear lesson about the agency problem of ruling. The disastrous experience of Qin might well have warned emperors about the high cost of state control via strict and elaborate laws. The fall of Qin might have been considered a conclusive falsification of the 'predator theory of the state'. Narrow self-interest backfired and the Chinese emperor learnt that to get the most from the 'slaves' (i.e. the whole Chinese population), the best way might be to set them free (until further notice). As noted by Fairbank *et al.* (1973): '. . . Qin . . . demonstrated the validity of one of Mencius's ideas: the government ultimately depends upon the tacit consent of the governed'.

From the point of view of the constituents, the instability and massacres during the Warring States period and the harsh governing style of Qin must have weighed very heavily on them. If only the state could have just left them alone, then they would have been very happy to sort out their own problems, even using private solutions in the form of *guanxi* to solve the enforcement problem. So the experience of Chou and Qin probably helped to make the subsequent system acceptable to both rulers and constituents.

7 The future of *guanxi*

Guanxi: persistence and change

Guanxi practice has been traced to the constraint of Chinese culture, which in turn has been shown to have developed in the context of the officially sanctioned ideology of Confucianism and the legal tradition of imperial China. The state's acquiescence in this method of social control and its acceptance by the constituents were shown to be maximizing. However, why has *guanxi* practice persisted after the end of imperial rule up until now and is it set to continue into the future?

While focus has been on cultural constraints (a discussion of the persistence and change of culture in general will be presented later), other factors have contributed to the persistence of *guanxi* practice among the Chinese. Basically, the most salient feature of *guanxi* practice is its comparatively lower cost in contract enforcement. This lower cost option is available because of the characteristics of Chinese culture. However, if options that are less costly than *guanxi* become available, then reliance on *guanxi* should fall.

Since the end of Qing rule until very recently nowhere in the world were the Chinese presented with a viable and lower-cost alternative to *guanxi* practice. In mainland China, Southeast Asia and Taiwan, there is either a lack of clear definition and enforcement of property rights by the state or the state is perceived to be corrupt or hostile to the Chinese. Where a seemingly viable alternative did become available in Hong Kong, the government has been regarded with less suspicion only in the last 25–30 years. Even in Hong Kong, due to the barrier of language and culture, the cost of using the law as an alternative means for contract enforcement was not at first thought to be low enough to justify its use. However, its use has gradually increased and it is generally perceived that the importance of *guanxi* has fallen in importance in Hong Kong relative to other places.

Culture in general has, by its nature, a strong tendency to perpetuate itself. However, this does not mean that it is immutable. Organizational institutionalists have provided a strong argument for the power of culture in conditioning the way we make sense of the world. The language, symbols and other institutions that are our creation also form the very basis for our thoughts. Our sense of 'reality' is in fact constructed by these cultural elements in such a way so as to fool us into believing that this is the only and universal way of seeing things, such that culture constrains how most people perceive, interpret and predict the world. Consequently the large majority of people take a dogmatic view of the ideas that they unconsciously hold and are in general incapable of rising above them to consider alternatives. This 'blinding effect' of culture is an important argument for its persistence.

Thus, Zucker (1991), an organizational institutionalist, wrote:

> It is argued here that internalization, self-reward, or other intervening processes need not be present to ensure cultural persistence because social knowledge once institutionalized exists as a fact, as part of objective reality, and can be transmitted directly on that basis . . . Each individual is motivated to comply because otherwise his actions and those of others in the system cannot be understood; the fundamental process is one in which the moral becomes the factual.

Such are the strong arguments for the persistence and self-perpetuating nature of culture. They account for the persistence of Chinese culture even though the official sanction by the state of Confucianism has either fallen in importance or totally reversed in the various countries and areas inhabited by the Chinese since the end of Qing rule. However, the problem with such arguments is that they accommodate no mechanism for allowing culture to change. They are thus presented as if culture is immutable. However, cultural changes do occur, albeit slowly, and if we are to predict the future of *guanxi* practice, then some understanding of the mechanism by which culture changes is essential.

One possible way culture is changed is when a diversity of cultures exists concomitantly. When confronted with such diversity, people may reconsider their own ideas and possibly revise them. In fact, even though there are great similarities in the views that different people of the same culture hold about the world, they are by no means identical. The greater the cultural diversity, say in a cosmopolitan city, the greater chance that reflections would bring about changes. A more relativist or tentative position may be adopted by many people.

If culture is understood to be concepts held by the general population, then another important moment when they might reconsider their concepts may be when their expectations about the world based on such concepts do not materialize. It must, of course, be admitted that instances where things do not turn out as expected do not always mean that a person would switch beliefs. All sorts of *ad hoc* theorizing and tautological arguments are available to protect one's beliefs, especially given the great complexity of the world, so cultural change is not easy. The argument is just that it is not impossible. The bottom line is the evolutionary argument, which, based on real forces, would mean that those with relatively superior theories would have a better chance of survival.

The arguments in explanation of why *guanxi* has flourished in China for contract enforcement as a substitute for civil law do not mean that *guanxi* will always serve this purpose in China. Conditions change, culture changes; so what is the future for *guanxi* in China in the long term? Such a prediction needs consideration of the present Chinese state, present day factors affecting cultural change and technical demands for more formalism.

More formalism – construction contracts

In the early years of China's reforms, cultural differences could be clearly seen between the PRC attitude to construction contracts and the contents of Western types of contract. The traditional PRC contract envisages two parties 'working together in a spirit of cooperation and equality using their best endeavours to carry out the state's construction projects efficiently and economically'. The Western type of contract has always anticipated a situation far short of complete identity of interest between the parties, whose relationship could become adversarial under commercial pressure. It attempts to set down a fully comprehensive schedule of rules governing the rights, obligations and remedies of the parties, to forestall disputes.

In contrast to the extremely detailed and legalistic Western style contracts, PRC contracts traditionally used to contain a few pages of simple contract terms and conditions that set out the intentions of the parties in a concise and practical manner in the expectation that each party would carry out its obligations in the best way that it could. Documents were often characterized by what appeared to others to be distinctly non-legalistic terms such as 'all items not found in this contract will be deliberated and decided upon in a spirit of mutual understanding and trust'. However in the years since the modernization began, the PRC's transition towards a socialist market economy has resulted in exposure to Western contracting methods and the contracts, even some of those used for indigenous projects (as opposed to joint ventures), have moved much closer in style and content to those found in Hong Kong.

(Compiled from: Walker, A., Levett, D. and Flanagan, R. *China: Building for Joint Venture*, Hong Kong: Hong Kong University Press, 1998)

The Chinese state now

Great importance has been placed on the state providing a structure of property rights under which its people transact business and attention has been drawn to the free-rider problem, which makes it difficult to organize people for the purpose of initiating property right changes. The major question is, will the present Chinese government be willing to institute reforms in its legal system to provide a comparatively lower cost alternative to *guanxi* as a way to enforce contracts? Ostensively, it is very improbable because the cost to the government is huge. What is of major significance is that to make the courts credible adjudicators they must be independent and protected from state intervention. This means that the state must give up some of its absolute power to the court and must be willing to subject itself to the rulings of the court. Even if the state gives up only its power to adjudicate economic disputes, this is still very costly because of its great involvement in the economy in terms of its state enterprises, collectives and other enterprises indirectly controlled by the government, party and military units. In addition are the costs of technicalities, for example drafting appropriate contract laws and building up a respectable and competent legal profession.

However, this does not mean that the government will never be willing to give up any power in order to make such property right reforms. The English crown gradually gave up many of its powers and often not as a result of violent struggles. If the ruler is able to share in the overall growth of the economy that results from such reforms or if the cost and risk of sticking to the original system is even higher than instituting a change, then proposing such property right reforms becomes viable. Answers to these questions in China depend on the interplay between the leadership of government, competitors outside the state, the ruling elite within the Communist Party who are also competitors of the rulers inside the state, the agents of the leaders and the constituents.

It seems that the present PRC leadership, unlike their imperial counterparts, is faced with a myriad of competitors both inside and outside the state. Outside the state are the potential military threats from other countries such as the USA, Russia, India, etc.

Economically, China is dependent on the developed countries, which include the USA, Europe and Japan, particularly following accession to the World Trade Organization. From time to time, China also has to consider potentially disruptive moves by Taiwan. In terms of economic dependence, there is a strong need for China to develop economically to gain greater autonomy. This urge is much stronger than it was in the past under the emperors. Economic development is even more urgent than meeting the military challenge of other states. This is so not just because recent wars conducted by the USA, such as those against Iraq, have clearly shown that they are battles of technology and that technological superiority is gained through economic wealth. More importantly, economic development could help avoid armed conflicts in the first place. For example, there is a much greater likelihood of a peaceful re-unification with Taiwan – one of the most difficult, yet important tasks for the PRC leadership – if China enjoys rapid economic development and the Taiwanese have a chance to share in the fruits of this development. Based on these considerations, the Chinese leadership should be stimulated to develop a property rights structure that lowers transaction costs and promotes economic development. Based on this argument, there is great motivation for the state to continue to improve the legal system.

China's economy

China's economy, the world's second-largest (measured at purchasing-power parity), has been gradually liberalising and expanding since Deng Xiaoping introduced market reforms 20 years ago. In 2001 the country joined the World Trade Organization. China now runs a trade surplus with the United States; it has also begun developing a high-tech industry and cleaning up state banks (many of which are drowning in non-performing loans). Foreign firms, dreaming of China's 1.3 billion potential consumers, invested $57 billion in China in 2003; metal producers in particular are booming by supplying China's demand.

continued

But growth is putting pressure on China's infrastructure: pollution is rife, health care strains rural resources, and the pension system lacks funds. A lack of labour mobility has led to high levels of unemployment, especially in the north-east, and protests by impoverished workers.

Wen Jiabao, the prime minister, hopes to address workers' concerns by cutting farmers' taxes and giving them better medical care and education. Still, the economy's recent growth – 9.1% in 2003 and an annualized 9.8% in the first the quarter of 2004 – has been such that fears of overheating have led the government to discourage banks from lending and try to tighten the housing market. The government is also under foreign pressure to let the undervalued yuan appreciate, which would hurt exports.

(From Economist.com, 10 September 2004)

The increasing role of private and collective enterprises

The structure of China's secondary industry changed fundamentally during the 1980s. Until 1978 output was dominated by large state-owned enterprises (SOEs). Since then much of the boom in manufacturing output has been produced by 'collective' enterprises under the aegis of local governments – particularly the township and village enterprises (TVEs) – or, increasingly, by private entrepreneurs or foreign investors, either in wholly owned enterprises or in joint ventures with Chinese interests. By 2002 the share of state-owned and state-holding enterprises in gross industrial output value had shrunk to 41%. However, state-owned companies, controlled by economic ministries in Beijing, taken in isolation represented only 16% of industrial output. State-holding enterprises may control large numbers of state firms, and are not 100% state-owned.

(From the Economist Intelligence Unit, Source: Country profile, 9 February 2004)

As for competitors inside the state, the situation is less clear. The general public does not elect the leadership. It seems safe to suppose that an elite group of several hundred to several thousand senior party members who occupy key positions in the military, party and the government organs have some say in the election of the leadership, but most power is still concentrated in the ultimate leader. There is considerable opaqueness in the distribution of power and it is fair to say that even those within the elite group are not sure who, at any point in time, has how much say.

If we consider the nature of the present leadership whose firm grip on power has not been doubted by most political commentators, the situation is optimistic. Such a firm grip on power provides incentives for making long-term investments in property rights reforms that benefit the whole state because the leadership is more certain to share the benefits of economic growth.

However, if we consider the opaqueness of the distribution of power within the ruling elite as well as the uncertainties in the way the leaders are elected/selected or removed, then the situation may not be so conducive to the leadership instituting property rights structures that enhance the wealth of the state as a whole. Doubts are raised about the ability of the leadership to share in overall economic growth as well as in whether the leadership will rule long enough to enjoy the fruits of its investment in property rights reforms. In which case there would be little incentive to make such an investment. Typically, behaviour in such a situation would be for the leadership to squeeze out as much wealth as possible in the short run at the expense of the state as a whole.

This may not be a concern with a stable leadership but if the leadership loses it grip on power then the problems associated with an opaque and uncertain leadership selection mechanism will become a reality. An ensuing power struggle will divert attention from such long-term economic development issues. If the subsequent leadership is weak then the elite group that put this leadership in place will have a great influence on any property rights structure. Usually this elite group of supporters would demand rewards in the form of privileges and special rights as individual members of this group and would be very unsure as to whether they could enjoy economic benefits by way of a general improvement in a property rights structure. Such a situation is detrimental to the development of a formal low transaction cost structure. However, because of the secretive way power is distributed and seized in totalitarian states, predictions about leadership and policy changes are notoriously difficult.

As for the agents of the ruler, the situation is also very different for today's leaders compared with the emperor. Selection is no longer based on an understanding of Confucian classics. It is also not based on an understanding of Marxist-Leninist thought as it was during communist rule before the Cultural Revolution, although allegiance to the Communist Party is still essential. Instead, knowledge of technical subjects is emphasized. The ideological inculcation of Confucianism that favours personalism through an examination system that controls the most important route for upward mobility is now over. The emphasis on formal knowledge leads away from *guanxi* coordination towards formal, explicit and clear-cut rules.

As for the size of the bureaucracy, it is much greater than in imperial times following expansion since 1949 due to the need to establish a centrally planned economy. To reduce the bureaucracy to a more manageable size is not an easy task given the many functions that the government has taken up since 1949 and the problem of providing alternative jobs for those who are made redundant within such a large population. If the size of the bureaucracy is not drastically reduced in the foreseeable future, the leadership has to establish ways to control it.

An emphasis on formalism is one possible way out. The experience of the Hong Kong government in controlling its bureaucracy through a formalistic system shows that this is possible. A move towards Weberian style bureaucracy measures means less personalism and more explicit rules, which is at least the first step towards a property rights system that relies more on legal means.

However, the large bureaucracy itself might have quite the opposite inclination. Formalism might be what the leadership wants but whether it can succeed is another matter. Consider for example the question of who is to supervise the execution of this increased control over the bureaucracy and who is to supervise the supervisors. What works for Hong Kong will not necessarily work for China because of the sheer size of the country. The high transaction cost of controlling the agents results in abuse of power and corruption among the agents. It might be speculated that one possible reason for Mao Zedong to launch the Cultural Revolution was concern for losing his control over his agents. So just as illegal organizations such as the mafia are often coordinated through personal connections because the law cannot be used as an agreement enforcer, a corrupt bureaucracy will also resort to personal connections as a means of organization. The effect is by no means limited to a state bureaucracy. The illegal obtaining of special rights by the private sector by bribery means that it too has to rely on non-legal measures for coordination, at least for that part that deals with the government. This factor supports the continued importance of *guanxi*. However, given the waning of Confucianism as a generally accepted ideology, the nature of *guanxi* will change.

When challenges from constituents are considered, a positive factor in favour of a reform of the property rights structure is found. This, ironically, is because the ruling Communist Party faces the danger of losing its legitimacy to rule following the numerous bloody political movements since 1949, the 4 June incident and the subsequent embracing of 'socialism with Chinese characteristics', that most inside China would take to mean capitalism, thus signifying the giving up of communism – the brand name for the ruling party. The emperors in imperial times always enjoyed the 'Mandate of Heaven'; as conferred by the state ideology of Confucianism. In those days, this ideology never lost its power to hold the minds of the subjects. With the disillusionment and abandonment of communism, the party's inculcation of a state ideology today is extremely difficult, if not impossible. One way to suppress opposition by the subjects is to 'bribe' them with economic benefits. Property rights reform is one important way to achieve this. Deng Xiaoping and the PRC government enjoyed much public support even after the Cultural Revolution exactly because the property rights reforms he instituted brought enormous economic benefits to the people.

Whether the state will move closer towards a property rights structure that makes legal solutions less costly and so lowers reliance on
guanxi is uncertain. If the leadership has more confidence in its grip
on power, the balance may tip towards more property rights reform
that will favour more legal means of contract enforcement, which
will see the importance of *guanxi* gradually wane.

Chinese law – modern developments

In the late Qing dynasty there was a concerted effort to establish
legal codes based on European models. Because of the German
victory in the Franco-Prussian War and because Japan was used
as the model for political and legal reform, the law codes which
were adopted were modelled closely after those of Germany.
These legal codes were then adopted by the new Republican
government but, because of the general disorder due to war-
lordism, they were not effectively put into practice.

Law in the People's Republic of China (mainland China) contem-
plates both a formal system of social control by the a legal system
and a complementary system of informal social control. This is
derived both from traditional principles of Confucianism and from
socialist theory.

After the communist victory in 1949, the People's Republic of
China (PRC) quickly abolished the Republic's legal codes and
attempted to create a system of socialist law copied from the
Soviet Union. With the rift with the Soviet Union and the Cultural
Revolution all legal work was suspected of being counter-
revolutionary and the legal system completely collapsed.

With the start of the Deng Xiaoping reforms, the need for
reconstructing a legal system to restrain abuses of official authority and revolutionary excesses was answered. In 1982, the
National People's Congress adopted a new state constitution
that emphasized the rule of law under which even party leaders
are theoretically held accountable. This reconstruction was done

in piece-meal fashion. Typically, temporary or local regulations would be established and after a few years of experimentation, conflicting regulations and laws would be standardized.

Since 1979, when the drive to establish a functioning legal system began, more than 300 laws and regulations, most of them in the economic area, have been promulgated. The use of mediation committees, informed groups of citizens who resolve about 90 per cent of the PRC's civil disputes and some minor criminal cases at no cost to the parties, is one innovative device. There are more than 800,000 such committees in both rural and urban areas.

Legal reform became a government priority in the 1990s. Legislation designed to modernize and professionalize the nation's lawyers, judges, and prisons was enacted. The 1994 Administrative Procedure Law allows citizens to sue officials for abuse of authority or malfeasance. In addition, the criminal law and the criminal procedures laws were amended to introduce significant reforms. Criminal procedures reforms also encouraged establishment of a more transparent, adversarial trial process. Subsequently, the enactment of laws has gained pace so that, whilst China is still some way from a fully developed and functioning legal system, more people and businesses are resorting to law as a way of resolving disputes.

(Compiled from: www.worldwidewebfind.com/encyclopedia/en/wikipedia/c/ch/chinese_law.html, (accessed June 2004))

Cultural change

The Confucian culture or ideology is an important constraint on the behaviour of the Chinese and is highly significant in enabling *guanxi* to act as a coordination mechanism and substitute for contract law. However, ideologies are not immutable. Nevertheless, whilst Confucianism has not been sanctioned as the state ideology for many years, the Chinese still display many characteristics that show that they still carry with them the Confucian codes, although in a weaker form. What prompts reconsideration of ideology is finding that what is expected based on the ideology is not borne out in reality, either through experience, observation of other people's experience or knowledge of different ideologies.

Although the adoption and maintenance of a Confucian culture has been persistent, it has suffered a number of important setbacks. The incompetence of the Chinese state in the face of Western aggression in the nineteenth century cast doubts on Confucian learning. There seemed to be other kinds of learning which might be more useful. The Confucian ideology suffered another heavy blow after the communists took power. Consequently, Confucianism was considered a remnant of feudalism and was blamed for China's backwardness. This was convincing because of the bitter experiences of the Chinese throughout the nineteenth century until the communist victory in 1949 during which time the Chinese people suffered both foreign aggression and civil war. After 1949 the mutual distrust that developed among the Chinese people during the various political movements when they were encouraged to betray their family members and friends by disclosing their 'wrongdoings' will also have weakened the ties which are regarded as vital for social order by Confucianists. After 1979, the emphasis on material benefits has further weakened Confucian ideals.

The one-child policy, enforced since the early 1980s, is also expected to have far reaching effects in moving the Chinese away from Confucianism. It means that children of the younger generation have no brothers or sisters. This also means that there will be no aunts, uncles, cousins, nieces and nephews. These are important bonds within the Confucian ideology. With children in short supply, the nature of the relationship between children and parents will also be dramatically different. The great increase in the 'bargaining power' of children means that parents are much less willing to subject their children to the rather harsh training, upbringing and inculcation of Confucian ideology. These children will have very little experience of interacting (fighting, arguing, negotiating, making deals, cooperating) with their peers. Such experience is vital to their training in *renqing* rules and in techniques for developing relationships that are both personal and instrumental and which characterize *guanxi* relationships.

Thus it is predicted that Confucianism as an ideology will continue to wane. But what will take its place and will this substitute provide *guanxi* with the kind of support provided by Confucianism?

At first it seemed that communism would replace Confucianism as the dominant ideology but this was not to be because of the bitter experiences of incessant extreme political movements from 1949 to 1976, particularly the Cultural Revolution. Expectations were met with disillusionment. Then, following the Cultural Revolution, when there was talk of a crisis of faith in the Communist Party, Deng Xiaoping initiated far-reaching reforms to the property rights structure following his return to power in 1979. The state argued such reforms were in conformity with the basic tenets of the Communist Party by saying that China was still at its early stage of socialism when many different forms of property structure could co-exist. The term 'Socialism with Chinese characteristics' was coined in the early 1990s to justify the imposition of private property rights reforms. By this time, the Chinese had been exposed to a whole range of ideologies and it was likely that they would be much more sceptical than before about what to believe.

Since the beginning of the 'Open Door Policy' in 1979, the Chinese have been exposed to the diversity of the outside world through the media as well as by direct contact, including overseas trips, overseas studies, overseas business, cooperation in joint venture companies, etc. These have opened the eyes of many Chinese. When they encountered and saw what they did not previously expect they were prompted to reconsider their own belief systems.

The scepticism of the Chinese towards ideology in general and their exposure to a diversity of cultures is likely to mean that there will not be a culture that commands the level of homogeneity previously ascribed to Confucianism. The waning of Confucianism, scepticism about belief systems and heterogeneity in culture will make using *guanxi* to enforce contracts more costly.

The pressure for more formalism

Besides the state's direction of property rights reform and the people's culture, the comparative advantage of *guanxi* needs to be assessed against more formal means of coordinating cooperation in business and industry that takes advantage of the current level of technology. Whilst there are some economies of scale in using the same personal cooperative relationships, since the nineteenth century technical developments leading to mass production, which does not rely on such relationships to such an extent, have enjoyed great progress. Expansion in world trade and increased income in China itself have also meant that markets are becoming much bigger than before, so the ability to exploit economies through mass production has a definite competitive edge. Thus economies of scale based on technical dimensions have enjoyed comparatively greater progress than specialization based on identity, which is the hallmark of *guanxi*. This is not favourable to *guanxi* for a number of reasons.

First, mass production requires the cooperation of a large number of people. With firms of this size, the transaction costs of formal means of control and coordination, though high, will still be lower than using personal connections. For example, cooperation with one person cannot be duplicated for another person and explicit and detailed policies of the whole firm have to be established to avoid misunderstanding between production units.

Also, mass production means that there is a much greater need for financing. To satisfy a financing need on this scale, loans from friends and relatives are not likely to be adequate, nor would it always be enough to form partnerships. To pool funds more readily business practice in the Western world is to issue shares to the public to invite people and institutions with excess funds to become shareholders of limited liability companies, to raise loans from financial institutions and to issue bonds to the public bond markets. All these factors necessitate more formalism. To introduce limited liability companies to reduce risks for shareholders requires legal developments in company law. A whole new set of rules to define business cooperation beyond simple trust is necessary. To issue shares and bonds to the public or to request loans from banks also means that personal connections become relatively unimportant; applicants are appealing to a group of people whom they may not know at all. Formal rules have to be used to guarantee that there is congruence in mutual expectation about the nature of the cooperation as well as what is going to happen if the cooperation breaks down.

An important event some years ago, which continues to have far reaching effects on the cost of using *guanxi*, was the 1997 Asian financial crisis. Many investors found it an important lesson in the need for more formalism and transparency. Before the crisis, dependence on trust in personal relationships instead of formal means of control meant that there was a lack of transparency for many companies listed on the Asian stock markets. This delayed the recognition of their problems and greatly magnified the crisis. This experience amounted to a refutation of the Asian way of relying mainly on trust and personal connections in doing business. The great pain that has resulted could cause a paradigm shift in this regard. International investors are likely to continue to become much more wary of companies that lack a formal way of reporting their status as well as their relationships with other individuals and firms and hence much less willing to invest. As a result, *guanxi* has become much more costly.

An illustration of the effect of the Asian financial crisis was the downfall of China's Guangdong International Trust and Investment Corporation (GITIC). The Chinese government's refusal to shoulder GITIC's debts and its insistence that the case be dealt with strictly according to the law demonstrates vividly China's recognition that *guanxi* is too costly and that it is more beneficial to move towards the rule of law.

In conclusion

As a result of analysing the state's incentive for developing the legal system to provide a lower cost alternative for *guanxi*, the answer is a cautious 'yes'. In analysing cultural change to assess whether the cost of continuing the use of *guanxi* itself will rise, the answer is 'yes'. Finally, in analysing the current status of technical development and the mass market to assess whether more formal means of coordination to take advantage of this technology has a comparative advantage over *guanxi*, the answer is 'yes'.

Manacling the mandarins

Extracts from *The Economist* print edition of 19 August 2004

China's powerful bureaucrats have lost a lawsuit

An obscure legal dispute about trademarks may signal a turning point in China's long march toward the rule of law. In the past month, Chinese legal experts have been unusually excited by a court judgment, little noticed outside the country, whereby an arm of China's national government was successfully sued by a private firm in a Chinese court. This may be the first time that any agency of the national government has lost a lawsuit, and the judgment is a direct result of recent legal changes brought about as a result of China joining the World Trade Organization (WTO) in 2001. Similar lawsuits challenging other arms of the government are likely. If some of these succeed, China's courts could end up providing an independent check on the almost unfettered power of bureaucrats, transforming the legal landscape for firms operating there.

In a country where trademarks are still widely violated, the case may seem a trifle esoteric to many business people. But in fact it fits a pattern all too typical across China's vast government bureaucracy, in which agencies blithely issue self-serving regulations. Until now, these have been free of any independent review. One reason the trademark bureau was reluctant to let a law firm file a trademark application was that this business has been confined to trademark agencies, most of whose fees flow to the bureau's parent ministry.

Also significant, say Chinese lawyers, is the fact that the Beijing court seemed to sit on the case until a new administrative licensing law took effect on July 1st. This was passed as part of the Chinese government's efforts to meet WTO requirements and to rein in its own bureaucrats by making administrative procedures more transparent and accountable. The law seems to have had an instant effect, emboldening the Beijing judges to rule against the trademark bureau. If other judges follow their lead, China's bureaucrats will no longer be a law unto themselves.

So it is predictable that *guanxi* will gradually fall in importance and that there will be a gradual development in the legal structure in China to allow an alternative to emerge for reducing transaction costs in business cooperation. To place a time frame on this development is extremely difficult. Slowly is probably the safe answer.

In conclusion, it should also be pointed out that the high level of generality in the explanation of *guanxi* means that diversity in Chinese culture as well as in *guanxi* practice, both over time and across geographic regions, have been ignored. There are differences in the practice of *guanxi* among the Chinese in mainland China, Taiwan, Hong Kong and overseas. There are also some differences in their culture, even though all can be regarded as basically Confucian. The property rights systems that are offered as a substitute for *guanxi* also differs between these places and this will also affect the importance and characteristics of *guanxi*. Such differences, besides being of interest in their own right, can also throw light on *guanxi* through comparing and contrasting such individual differences. For example, the historical, institutional and cultural background of Hong Kong is quite different from Taiwan. The *guanxi* practice is also different.

Also Confucianism has been used as a proxy for culture, but it must be admitted that Chinese culture is obviously broader than Confucianism. Cultural and ideological inculcation are often transmitted through institutions. Because of the highly general approach taken by this book, only a few examples of this critical link, such as the examination system in imperial China, have been referred to. However, many other important institutions, especially those centring on the family and business practices, have not been referred to. For example, trade associations called *huiguans* were quite common in the late Qing and some of them have served in a more institutionalized way as third party guarantors of contracts between private individuals. In a way this is a more formalized form of *guanxi*. Consideration of such institutions in the transmission of ideology as well as constraints on behaviour so as to make *guanxi* a useful transaction cost economizer could enrich our understanding of *guanxi* and Chinese business practice.

The cost of maintaining the *guanxi* system in China can only increase because of the many sources of influence coming from all parts of the world. Confucianism is out of touch with the world as it is today. What it has to counter is the dominant ideology of individualism and calculative rationality. Moreover, given the dominant ideology of individualism, the actual pattern of thinking can differ greatly. Homogeneity of ways of looking at the world, let alone Confucianism in particular, is difficult to achieve. So to think that reliance on the homogeneous Confucianist culture can continue as a means of contract enforcement is impractical. Active efforts to inculcate a homogeneous culture will not be effective.

Furthermore, *guanxi* is increasingly being used to disguise corruption, which is not beneficial to a country in the long run. As *guanxi* ceases to be a viable alternative for reducing transaction costs, what is needed is more formalism and less personalism. So what the government can do is to actively develop an alternative low-cost system for enforcing property rights contracts. This is particularly urgent because of the problem of continuing reliance on *guanxi* referred to above. Such a system needs to include, not only the legal system with an independent judiciary and a properly drawn civil law, but also a well respected private legal profession. Other independent professions that can provide independent valuations for commercial purposes, such as accountancy and the real estate professions, must also be encouraged to develop so that formalization of contracts in writing and an impersonal system for enforcement are possible.

Guanxi in action

Some examples of Western business's experience with guanxi

Drugmakers find that *guanxi* endures

Beijing's entry into the World Trade Organization three years ago was supposed to make China more a rule-based system, where *guanxi* would have far less influence, and also improve its legal system to make its rules easier for companies to understand. Yet *guanxi* remains important in China. Just ask Andreas Tschirky, head of the new research centre in Shanghai for the Roche Group, the Swiss pharmaceutical company. He says the local and central governments understand the importance of beefing up protection for intellectual property-rights (IPR) – and one sign of their commitment is the relationships that Roche now has with their representatives.

'We have a specific person in the Shanghai government to whom we can address all of our issues' says Tschirky, who adds that Roche has 'direct access' to officials from central government.

Others in the industry also say they've had encouraging contacts with officials. That's one reason that many drugmakers are focusing on the Chinese market, which is among the top 10 in the world today and will probably grow to the top three within the next ten years. 'I'm optimistic', says Steen Kroyer, head of China and Hong Kong for AstraZeneca. 'We get strong support from the central government'.

(Compiled from: http://www.businessweek.com/bwdaily/dnflash/dec2004/nf2004127_9786_db065.htm, (accessed May 2005))

BP builds *guanxi*

Cultural differences can give rise to real business issues, as BP discovered during negotiations with Fuhua, prospective partner

continued

in the $400 million Zhuhai chemicals joint venture. Negotiating positions became so entrenched that the project was cancelled, much to the frustration of all concerned.

As an organization building a multi-billion oil, gas, and chemical business in the country, diversity and inclusion is a high priority in BP China today – as the president of BP China, Gary Dirks confirms:

> The cultural dimension is critical to understanding how business is done, how approvals are obtained, and what are the priorities and expectations of our joint venture partners. We already have many good young Chinese nationals on our team, but we are determined to recruit more national staff and develop their potential as future leaders.

Linda Shum, president of Zhuhai Chemical Company, was born in Indonesia of Chinese parents, so appreciates many of the cultural nuances – 'The Chinese have 20 different ways of smiling, indicating anything from absolute delight to down-right fury'. It was Linda who rescued the negotiations with Fuhua. 'The only way to recover the relationship was for top BP leaders to meet their Chinese counterparts face-to-face', she recalls. 'We solved the situation in a very Chinese way by apologizing, explaining our reasons for the cancellation, and promising to build a bigger and better plant'.

The company hosted a seminar at Tsing Hua University at which academics and government officials were invited to share their views of the future with a group of senior executives from BP. 'China through China's Eyes' was a unique opportunity for east and West to meet in common forum of openness, and view the opportunities and challenges ahead from a common perspective.

'I found it truly excellent, with frankness to the discussions that really surprised me,' said Linda Shum. 'There's a special word in

China for that kind of relationship – we call it "*guanxi*", and we're determined to build good "*guanxi*" in BP China'.

Compiled from: http://www.bp.com (accessed May 2005)

Getting results through *guanxi*

I met Mark Wang the day he resigned from the office. He had been working there for half a year as a sales representative. Before we met up he had expressed his feeling of difficulty working for a Scandinavian company in an email: 'I have some problem on the communication with the management team. Maybe you can help me find a way to solve it. I am going to learn Scandinavian culture and language. Maybe you are a good tutor.' The problem is the extent of using *guanxi*. Wang has been hired partly because of his *guanxi*. The human resources manager explains to me that employees in the sales department are hired, not only on the basis of their personal abilities, but also on basis of their network of customers.

Wang operates using his *guanxiwang* – *guanxi* network doing business. To do market research he, in a sense, employs a number of agents. These agents do not make deals for him, but they use their contacts to obtain information. Wang finds these services necessary, for example in relation to government policy. He says that the government controls the stock-market. This makes it important to know the government preferences.

> In order to keep in touch with government policy you need to have *guanxi* with someone in touch with the central government, someone who knows what the government policy will be next. The government may, for example, show an interest in the cable-tv market. They will open up for investment in this market by loosening restrictions. If you know this is coming you will be able to take advantage of it. If you do not keep up to date on government policy you may get surprises.

continued

The relationship with the agents takes the form of friends, at least this is the ideal. And in this regard its resemblance to other types of *guanxi* networks becomes more obvious. The relation is no longer one of pure instrumental purpose, but has a very clear affectionate side to it.

Once you've made friends they'll help you. They'll do a lot of marketing jobs for you. They are not employees, but at the same time they still work for you, only they do different work. If they are really good friends they'll help you get a deal without having to get paid, then you'll help them get a deal later. That's how it works! In other cases you should pay them for all the work they do for you. No paying – no game! Everyone is a bit selfish. They work for their own good. You have to! The agents do marketing jobs for the company. The company needs more marketing people, the marketing department does not function. This is a huge problem! We could use employees with some contacts in the government. You need the agents, you can not do anything by yourself – even strong people need a guy's help. The company is too concerned about their reputation. I understand that they want to keep 'a clean face', but it doesn't give results in China. This is one of the company's major weaknesses, they don't pay enough attention to *guanxi*. As long as I get results the company should not be so concerned about how I get them. If you want to hire someone, you should trust them. You can't work when there is no trust. In the beginning the company was high on trust, but after a while they would start asking me about how everything was done, how I did the job, how I got the deal and such, there was no trust. I can't work for a company where there is no trust. Usually I don't like to tell, I shouldn't have to tell as long as I got the job done. In my old job I did not have to tell. I just showed the results.

Also the treatment of customers should be based on the notion of friendship. The customers will be part of your *guanxiwang* in the same way as the agents.

The customers are also human. They have a heart. First you need to open yourself to them as a friend. You build up a friendship. They are not customers, but friends. Yi hui *sheng*, er hui shou – first you're a stranger, then a friend. Second; how do you build up this relationship if you're a foreigner? It's hard.

To solve the task of getting good results, Mark Wang thinks it necessary to use a network of agents. Only by having *guanxi* through agents, or contacts in the government system, is the company able to get the information it needs to run successfully.

Extracted from Stallemo, M., 'Guanxi in a changing Shanghai', presented at the Workshop China's Challenges at the Turn of the 21st Century, June 2001, available on: http://www.helsinki.fi/nacs/maren _stallemo.htm (accessed May 2005)

Guanxi through long-term business relationships

In China, any business relationship should be considered from a long-term view. To maintain a long-term business relationship, one must reciprocate. One never knows when one will be in trouble and a friend in need is a friend indeed. This reflects the necessity of reciprocity. The experience of a joint venture in Beijing offers a typical example of reciprocity. In the early 1990s one of the suppliers of cashmere in Inner Mongolia had funding problems when planning its technical transformation. The joint venture, a producer of cashmere knitwear, was approached for help. Considering the long-term relationship, the joint venture decided to provide funding for the supplier. In the mid-1990s, the market for cashmere knitwear heated up and the price of cashmere raw material rocketed and, as a consequence, many cashmere knitwear producers had difficulty in absorbing the price rise and had to reduce production. The joint venture faced the same problem. However, the supplier in Inner Mongolia did not forget the help that the joint venture had given and offered to supply cashmere raw material at below market price. The joint

continued

venture not only survived the price rise in raw material, but also captured the market that their competitors left because of the price rise. The implication of this joint venture's experience is that the commitment to a good long-term business relationship and the obligations arising from such a relationship will survive market changes.

(Compiled from: http://www.bigtp.com/inf_3.html (accessed May 2005))

And examples of how it works in practice within China

Cold storage trucks

In order to ship fresh mushrooms to Germany in time for Christmas, a Sino-German joint venture firm in an eastern Chinese city had to borrow eight cold storage trucks from a food producer. Knowing that his trucks were the only suitable vehicles available in the town, the food producer asked for a price six times higher than the market price. Moreover he refused to bargain, even though he did not need those trucks at that time. After a few days of extensive search, the joint venture manager found out that the food producer was trying to get a contract from the airport to supply airline food. This Sino-German firm happened to have *guanxi* with the airport because the firm often shipped mushrooms by air. In a phone call to the airport, the Chinese manager of the joint venture firm asked for help in the truck rental issue. Soon the food producer agreed to negotiate, and later allowed the joint venture firm to rent his trucks at a reasonable price.

Repayment of a loan

A manager of a south China company signed a one year contract to lend money to a real estate developer. A year later he had difficulty getting his money back, in spite of the contract – a not uncommon occurrence in modern China. One day he happened to have lunch with a banker from a state bank, with which the company had long ago developed *guanxi*. When he described his dilemma, the banker suddenly recalled that his bank was considering a loan to the same developer. The firm manager (very happy to have this information), asked the banker to delay approving the loan. The banker agreed a few days later, the developer paid back the money in full.

(Ji Li and Philip C. Wright (1999) 'The Issue of Guanxi: Discrepancies, Reality and Implications', BRC Working Paper No. WP 99036, School of Business, Hong Kong Baptist University)

Notes

1 What is *guanxi*?

1   In the Wade-Giles system, *guanxi* is spelt as *kuan-hsi*. However, the former is much more popular. The latter is used mainly in Taiwan or by scholars from Taiwan. The transliteration system used in this book is based on Peking's pin-yin system.

2   For studies of the PRC, see for example Tai (1988), Brunner and Taoka (1977), Lee and Lo (1988), Lee (1997). For studies of Taiwan, see for example Numazaki (1996), Tu (1991), Lin (1991), Myers (1982), Hamilton and Biggart (1988/1997), Kao (1996), Winn (1994), DeGlopper (1995). For studies of Hong Kong, see for example Landa (1981), Omohundro (1983), Barton (1983), Limlingan (1986). For the use of *guanxi* for the Chinese in general, see for example Brunner *et al.* (1989), Hamilton *et al.* (1990).

3   Opportunism is a term used by transaction cost economists such as Williamson (1985) to describe human behaviour: 'By opportunism, I mean self-interest with guile. This includes but is scarcely limited to more blatant forms, such as lying, stealing, and cheating. Opportunism more often involves subtle forms of deceit. Both active and passive forms and both ex ante and ex post types are included.'

2 Explaining *guanxi*

1   Liang Chi-chao (1873–1929) in Liang Chi-chao (1936), *Rujia Zhexue* (The Confucian Philosophy), Shanghai: Chung-hua Shu-chu, as quoted by Hsieh (1967).

2   The other two are the *youxia* (knight-errantry) tradition, and the Buddhist notions of retribution.

3   Translated and quoted by Yang (1957).

4   Translated and quoted by Yang (1957).

5   In brief, Chandler's theory of organization form can be summarized thus: 'The rise of modern mass production required fundamental changes in the technology and organization of the process of production . . . [E]conomies came more from the ability to integrate and coordinate the flow of materials through the plant than from greater specialization and subdivision of the work within the plant.' This is because Chandler regarded 'high-speed throughput' as the most striking characteristic of mass production. With the huge capital investment in plants, there were 'increased pressures on the owners and managers to control their supplies of raw and semi-finished materials and to take over their own marketing and distribution.' With the need to integrate mass production and mass distribution, large multifunctional and multiunit firms resulted. Thus, large firms emerged to replace the small partnerships or family businesses that have long dominated the pre-industrial American economy. That is, Chandler argued for the technical superiority of administrative over market coordination under conditions of mass markets.

6   There is often confusion between transaction cost and an arrangement to reduce transaction cost. The arrangement to reduce transaction cost is itself costly, so the cost of this arrangement, as it is now the arrangement with the lowest cost, becomes the transaction cost. What is termed here as 'transaction cost' can thus also be interpreted as the cost of the best means to reduce transaction cost of the next best arrangement to achieve the exchange/transaction.

7   In fact, the importance of stability is analogous to the importance of a clear definition of rights and certainty about the system of enforcing contracts. Ultimately, it is a matter of how certain we are about our expectations; whether it is about if and how the contract would be performed, who really has the rights so that we are negotiating and exchanging with the right persons, or whether the person would behave in the consistent way we expect him or her to behave, in the absence of legally binding contracts.

8   See for example Wright (1957) and Fairbank *et al.* (1973).

3 Analysing *guanxi*

1   Arrow's words in a discussion as recorded in Hirshleifer (1982).

2   Paul David (1986) described how the highly inefficient QWERTY typewriter keyboard, the one we are now using, became the standard of the industry by the 1890s. This occurred despite the existence of many more efficient designs in which the most frequently typed letters

are on the home row. The QWERTY design was developed originally because the first typewriters were built in such a way that the lines being typed did not come into view until many lines of type later; consequently, key jams could not be detected until many lines consisting of a single letter and had already been typed. The QWERTY keyboard minimized the jam, an important feature at this time. Meanwhile, typing schools began to teach this keyboard, so that the large number of typists who carried this arrangement in their heads became an important consideration for businesses deciding which keyboard to purchase, just as the installed base of the QWERTY machine had to be taken into account by those deciding which keyboard to learn. As a result of these feedback effects, QWERTY became established as the technical standard, and was 'locked-in' by the large base of existing machines and users. By the 1890s, when this lock-in had occurred, the original rationale for QWERTY had disappeared because each line could be seen as it was typed; but the process could not be, and has not been, reversed.

5 The influence of law in imperial China

1 From Huan-nan-tzu (the Master of Huai-nan) and quoted by Bodde (1981). The book is an eclectic philosophical work, composed by scholars attached to the court of Liu An, Prince of Huan-nan who died in 122 BC.

2 See for example Keith (1994).

3 See for example Bodde (1981), Chen (1973), Unger (1976), Wu (1967).

4 This is a generally held view. See for example Wu (1967), MacCormack (1996), Bodde (1981).

5 Rulers of Yuan were of Mongol origin and had a culture foreign to traditional Chinese. Unlike the Qing rulers who also had a foreign culture, but who chose to integrate their culture with that of the Chinese, the Yuan rulers never attempted such integration.

6 Including Wu (1967), Van der Sprenkel (1977), Fairbank (1992), Bodde (1981), Chen (1973), MacCormack (1996).

7 There is an old saying from the *Book of Rites*: '*Xing bus hang da fu. Li bu xia shu ren*' ['The penal codes do not extend up to the officials' Li does not extend down to the common people'.] (*Book of Rites* I). The sentiment expressed in this dictum was never literally applied. Officials were punished by their rules, sometimes savagely. But while disregarding the inequity implied (and the possibility that this might express the wish of officials rather than that of Confucius himself), there is also the idea that *li* is a higher and more honourable way to

maintain order – to be applied to officials who are often *Jun Zi* ('gentlemen') as they are Confucian scholars themselves, and only when one is dealing with the mass, who presumably are uneducated and thus morally questionable, does the law have to be applied.

6 The rationality of the traditional Chinese legal and cultural systems

1   As noted by North (1981), there are two theories of the state: the contract theory (the state will strike a bargain with the constituents that will maximize the total wealth of both parties) and the predatory theory (the ruler will try to extract income from the constituents to maximize his own wealth, possibly to the detriment not only of the constituents but to the aggregate wealth of the ruler and constituents). North recognized that the two theories are not inconsistent, but the reasons he gave in his book is not convincing: 'It is the distribution of "violence potential" that reconciles them. The contract theory assumes an equal distribution of violence potential amongst the principals. The predatory theory assumes an unequal distribution'. It seems what reconciles them is not the 'distribution of violence potential', but the standard tools of economic analysis as propounded by Adam Smith – potential for gain from trade turns selfish individuals (a common assumption for economics as well as the predator theory) into people deeply concerned with other people's welfare. So the emperor, being a self-seeking individual himself, and knowing that a certain arrangement will increase the wealth of the constituents more than it will reduce his own, will certainly propose to 'sell' this arrangement to the constituents who would be asked to pay a sum greater than the ruler's potential loss; and the constituent *will agree* – because if this new arrangement generates more aggregate wealth, then the gain for the constituents will by definition exceed the minimum the ruler asks for. So what is maximizing for the whole will also be maximizing for the individuals: the rulers and the constituents. The *caveat* here is the huge transaction cost in making such a trade and this might prevent it from happening. So distribution of violence potential is a parameter (in the form of resources available to the ruler) in predicting the result of the bargain, but this should not prevent the cost/benefit analysis implicit in the 'contract theory' of the state from being the better analytical framework. In fact, even slave masters (who can be the ultimate 'predator') might find it worthwhile to grant freedom to the slave and then contract with them based on voluntary trade (see for example Barzel (1977)).

Bibliography

Acheson, J.M., ed. *Anthropology and Institutional Economics,* New York: University Press of America, 1992.

Akerlof, G. A., 'Loyalty Filters', *American Economic Review,* 73(1), March 1983.

Alchian, A.A., 'Uncertainty, Evolution and Economic Theory', *Journal of Political Economy,* 58(3), June 1950.

Axelrod, R., 'The Emergence of Cooperation Amongst Egoists', *American Political Science Review,* 75, 1981.

——, *The Evolution of Cooperation,* New York: Basic Books, 1984.

Baker, H., *Chinese Family and Kinship,* New York: Columbia University Press, 1979.

Barton, C.G., 'Trust and Credit: Some Observations regarding Business Strategies of Overseas Chinese Traders in South Vietnam' in Lim, L.Y.L. and Gosling, L.A.P., eds. *The Chinese in South East Asia: Volume 1, Ethnicity and Economic Activity,* Singapore: Maruzen, 1983.

Barzel, Y., 'An Economic Analysis of Slavery', *Journal of Law and Economics,* 20, April 1977.

——, *Economic Analysis of Property Rights,* Cambridge: Cambridge University Press, 1989.

Becker, G.S., 'Altruism, Egoism, and Genetic Fitness: Economics and Sociobiology', *Journal of Economic Literature,* 14(3), September 1976.

Benedict, R., *The Chrysanthemum and the Sword,* New York: Meridian, 1946.

Ben-Porath, Y., 'The F-connection: Family, Friends and Firms and the Organization of Exchange,' *Population and Development Review,* 6, 1980.

Berger, P. and Luckman, T., *The Social Construction of Reality: A Treatise in the Sociology of Knowledge,* London: Penguin, 1966.

Bian, Y. and Ang, S., 'Guanxi Networks and Job Mobility in China and Singapore', *Social Forces,* 75, 1997. Chinese translation published in *Foreign Sociology,* 4, 1999.

Biggart, N.W., 'Explaining Asian Economic Organization: Towards a Weberian Institutional Perspective', in Orr, M., Biggart, N. W., and

Hamilton, G.G., eds. *The Economic Organization of East Asia Capitalism,* Thousand Oaks, CA: Sage Publications, 1997.

—— and Hamilton, G.G., 'On the Limits of a Firm-Based Theory to Explain Business Networks: the Western Bias of Neoclassical Economics', in Nohria, N. and Eccles, R.G., eds. *Networks and Organizations: Structure, Form and Action,* Boston, MA: Harvard Business School Press, 1992.

Bodde, D., 'Basic Concepts of Chinese Law: the Genesis and Evolution of Legal Thought in Traditional China', in *Essays on Chinese Civilization,* Princeton, NJ: Princeton University Press, 1981.

Boisot, M.H., *Information Space: A Framework for Learning in Organizations, Institutions and Culture,* London and New York: Routledge, 1995.

Bonavia, D., *The Chinese,* London: Allen Lane, 1980.

Brunner, J.A. and Taoka, G.M., 'Marketing and Negotiation in the People's Republic of China: Perceptions of American Businessmen who Attended the 1975 Canton Trade Fair', *Journal of International Business Studies,* 8(2), Winter/Fall 1977.

——, Chan, J., Sun, C., and Zhou, N., 'The Role of *Guanxi* in Negotiation in the Pacific Basin, *Journal of Global Marketing,* 3(2), 1989.

Carmody, D.L. and Carmody, J.T., *Eastern Ways to the Centre: An Introduction to Asian Religions,* Belmont, CA: Wadsworth, 1983.

Chan, W.T., *Source Book of Chinese Philosophy,* Princeton, NJ: Princeton University Press, 1963.

Chandler, A., *The Visible Hand: the Managerial Revolution in American Business* Cambridge, MA: Belknap Press, 1977.

Chen, P.M., *Law and Justice: The Legal System in China 2400 BC to 1960 AD,* New York: Dunellen, 1973.

Cheng, C.Y., 'Chinese Philosophy: A Characterization', in Naess, A. and Hannay, A., eds. *Invitation to Chinese Philosophy,* Oslo: Universitetsforlaget, 1972.

Chiao, C., '*Guanxi*: a Preliminary Conceptualization', in Yan, K. and Wne, C., eds. *The Sinicization of Social and Behavioural Science Research in China,* Taipei: Academica Sinica, 1982 (in Chinese).

Ch'u, T., *Law and Society in Traditional China,* Sorbonne: École Pratique Des Haute Études, 1961.

Chu, G. and Ju, Y., *The Great Wall in Ruins: Cultural Change in China,* Honolulu: East West Centre, 1990.

Coase, R.H., 'The Nature of the Firm', *Economica,* n.s., 4, November 1937.

——, *The Firm, The Market and the Law,* Chicago, IL: University of Chicago Press, 1988.

Dahlman, C.J., 'The Problem of Externality', *The Journal of Economics,* 22, 1979.

Dannhaeuser, N., 'Evolution and Devolution of Downward Channel

Integration in the Philippines', *Economic Development and Cultural Change,* 29(3), 1981.

David, P.A., 'Understanding the Economics of QWERTY: The Necessity of History' in Parker, N.N., ed. *Economic History and the Modern Economist,* New York: Basil Blackwell, 1986.

De Mente, B.L., *Chinese Etiquette and Ethics in Business,* Lincolnwood, IL: NTC Business Books, 1992.

DeGlopper, D.R., *Lukang: Commerce and Community in a Chinese City,* Albany, NY: State University of New York Press, 1995.

DiMaggio, P., 'Culture and Economy' in Smelser, N.J. and Swedberg, R., eds. *The Handbook of Economic Sociology,* Princeton, NJ: Princeton University Press, 1994.

Dixit, A.K. and Nalebuff, B.J., *Thinking Strategically: the Competitive Edge in Business, Politics and Everyday Life,* New York: Norton, 1991.

Dürer, A., *Rhinoceros, woodcut,* New York Public Library, 1515.

Eberhard, W., *Guilt and Sin in Traditional China,* Berkeley and Los Angeles, CA: University of California Press, 1967.

Fairbank, J.K., Reischauer, E.O., and Craig A.M., *East Asia; Tradition and Transformation,* (revised edn), Boston, MA: Houghton Mifflin, 1973.

Fairbank, J.K., *China: A New History,* Cambridge, MA: Belknap Press of Harvard University Press, 1992.

Fei, X., *From the Soil: The Foundation of Chinese Society,* English translation by Hamilton, G.G., and Zheng, W., Berkeley, CA: University of California Press, 1943/1992.

Frank, R.H., 'If Homo Econimicus Could Choose His Own Utility Function, Would He Want One With a Conscience?', *American Economic Review,* 77(4), September 1987.

——, *Passions within Reason: the Strategic Role of the Emotions,* New York: W.W. Norton, 1988.

Ge, G. and Ting-Toomey, S., *Communicating Effectively with the Chinese,* Thousand Oaks, CA: Sage Publications, 1988.

Gombrich, E.H., *Art and Illusion: A Study in the Psychology of Pictorial Representation.* (5th edn), London: Phaidon Press, 1960/1977.

Hamilton, G.G., 'Why No Capitalism in China? Negative Questions in Historical, Comparative Research', *Journal of Developing Societies,* 1, 1985.

——, 'Patterns of Asian Capitalism: The Cases of Taiwan and South Korea', *East Asian Culture and Development Research Working Papers Series No. 28,* Davis, CA: Institute of Government Affairs, University of California, 1989.

—— and Biggart, N.W., 'Market Culture and Authority: A Comparative Analysis of Management Organization in the Far East,' *American Journal of Sociology, Special Supplement on the Sociology of the Economy,* 1988.

—— and Feenstra, R.C., 'Varieties of Hierarchies and Markets: An

Introduction', in Orru, M., Biggart, N.W. and Hamilton, G.G., *The Economic Organization of East Asia Capitalism*, Thousand Oaks, CA: Sage Publications, 1997.

——, Zeile, W. and Kim, W., 'The Network Structures of East Asian Economies', in Clegg, S.R., Redding, G.S. and Cartner, M., eds. *Capitalism in Contrasting Cultures*, Berlin: Walter de Gruyter,1990.

Hansen, V., *Negotiating Daily Life in Traditional China: How Ordinary People Used Contracts, 600–1400*, New Haven, CT: Yale University Press, 1995.

Hau, T., *The Study of Chinese Legal Tradition (Zhong hua fa xi yan jiu)*, Shanghai: Fudan University Press, 1997 (Chinese publication).

Heath, J., 'Rhinoceros in Africa', 1789 engraving from Bruce, J., *Travels to Discover the Source of the Nile, Vol. V*, G.G.J. and J. Robinson: Edinburgh, 1790.

Hirshleifer, J., 'Evolutionary Models in Economics and Law', in Zerbe, R.O. and Rubin, P.H., eds. *Research in Law and Economics, Vol. 4.* Greenwich, CT: JAI Press, 1982.

Hobbes, T., *The Leviathan*, Middlesex, UK: Penguin Books, 1651/1962.

Hsieh, Y., 'Filial Piety and Chinese Society', in Moore, C.A., ed. *The Chinese Mind: Essentials of Chinese Culture*, Honolulu: East West Centre Press, 1967.

Hsu, F.L.K., 'Suppression versus Repression: a Limited Psychological Interpretation of Four Cultures', *Psychiatry*, 12, 1949.

——, 'Psychological Homeostasis and Jen: Conceptual Tools for Advancing Psychological Anthropology', in Bohannan, L., ed. *American Anthropologist*, 73(1), 1971.

Jacobs, J.B., 'The Concept of *Guanxi* and Local Politics in a Rural Chinese Cultural Setting' in Greenblat, S., Wilson, R. and Wilson, A.A., eds. *Social Interaction in Chinese Society*, New York: Praeger, 1982.

Kao, C., 'Personal Trust in the Large Businesses in Taiwan: A Traditional Foundation for Contemporary Economic Activities', in Hamilton, G.G., ed. *Asian Business Networks*, Berlin: Walter de Gruyter, 1996.

Keith, R.C., *China's Struggle for the Rule of Law*, London: Macmillan, 1994.

King, A.Y., 'Kuan-hsi and Network Building: A Sociological Interpretation' *Daedalus*, 120(2), 1991.

——, 'The Analysis of *Renqing* in Human Relationships' in Yang, L., ed. *The Meaning of Reciprocity, Guarantee and Undertaking in Chinese Culture*, Hong Kong: The Chinese University Press, 1987.

Kipnis, A.B., *Producing Guanxi Sentiment, Self and Subculture in a North China Village*, Durham, NC: Duke University Press, 1997.

Kroeber, A. and Kluckhohl, A., 'Culture: A Critical Review of Concepts and Definitions', *Peabody Museum of American Archaeology and Ethnology* Vol. 47, Cambridge, MA: Harvard University Press, 1952.

Landa, J.T., 'A Theory of the Ethnically Homogeneous Middleman Group: A Institutional Alternative to Contract Law', *Journal of Legal Studies* Vol. X, June 1981.

——, 'The Political Economy of the Ethically Homogeneous Chinese Middlemen Group in Southeast Asia: Ethnicity and Entrepreneurship in a Plural Society' in Lim, L.Y.L. and Gosling, L.A.P., eds. *The Chinese in Southeast Asia: Vol.1, Ethnicity and Economic Activity,* Singapore: Maruzen, 1983.

Lee, K.H. and Lo, T.W., 'American Business People's Perception of Marketing and Negotiation in the PRC', *International Marketing Review,* Summer 1988.

Lee, T.V., *Contract, Guanxi and Dispute Resolution in China,* New York: Garland Publishing, 1997.

Leung, T., Wong, S. and Wong, Y.H., 'Hong Kong Businessmen's Perception of *Guanxi* in the PRC,' in *Proceedings: Conference on Asian Success and International Business Theory,* Hong Kong: Business School, University of Hong Kong, 1993.

Li, X. and Wu, Q., '*Guanxixue*: The Theory' in Zeng, C. and Wen, Z., eds. *Chinese Guanxi Study,* Hong Kong: Hong Kong Asia Pacific Research Institute, Chinese University of Hong Kong, 1996 (Chinese Publication).

Liang, C.C., *Rujia Zhexue (The Confucian Philosophy),* Shanghai: Chunghua, 1936 (Chinese Publication).

Limlingan, V.S., *The Overseas Chinese in ASEAN: Business Strategies and Management Practices,* Philippines: Vita Development Corporation, 1986.

Lin, P., 'The Social Sources of Capital Investment in Taiwan's Industrialization' in Hamilton, G.G., ed. *Business Networks and Economic Development in East and Southeast Asia,* Hong Kong: Centre of Asian Studies, University of Hong Kong, 1991.

Macauley, M.A., 'Civil and Uncivil Disputes in Southeast Costal China, 1723–1820' in Bernhardt, K. and Huang, P.C.C., eds. *Civil Law in Qing and Republican China,* Stanford, CA: Stanford University Press, 1994.

MacCormack, G., *The Spirit of Traditional Chinese Law,* London: The University of Georgia Press, 1996.

Mead, G. H., *Mind, Self and Society*, Chicago, IL: University of Chicago, 1934.

Myers, R.H., 'Customary Laws, Markets and Resource Transactions in Late Imperial China' in Ransom, R.L., ed. *Explorations in the New Economic History,* New York: Academic Press, 1982.

Nakamura, H., *Ways of Thinking of Eastern Peoples,* Honolulu: East West Centre Press, 1964. Revised English translation, edited by Wiener, P.P.

Needham, J., *The Shorter Science and Civilization in China,* Cambridge: Cambridge University Press, 1978 (abridged by Ronan, C.A.).

North, D.C., *Structure and Change in Economic History,* New York: Norton, 1981.

——, *Institutions, Institutional Change and Economic Performance,* Cambridge: Cambridge University Press, 1990.

—— and Thomas, R.P., *The Rise of the Western World: A New Economic History,* Cambridge: Cambridge University Press, 1973.

Numazaki, I., 'The Role of Personal Networks in the Making of Taiwan's *Guanxiqiye* (Related Enterprises)' in Hamilton, G.G., ed. *Asian Business Networks,* Berlin: Walker de Gruyter, 1996.

Olsen, M.J.R., 'Economics, Sociology and the Best of All Possible Worlds' *Public Interest,* Summer 1968.

Omohundro, J.T., 'Social Networks and Business Success for the Philippine Chinese', in Lim, L.Y.C. and Gosling, L.A.P., eds. *The Chinese in Southeast Asia.* Singapore Maruzen Asia, 1983.

Orru, M., Biggart, N.W. and Hamilton, G.G., eds. *The Economic Organization of East Asia Capitalism,* Thousand Oaks, CA: Sage Publications, 1997.

Pan, K., *Cheng-hsueh chu yen* (Comments on political issues), Shanghai: Kuan-ch'a She, 1948 (Chinese Publication).

Patten, C., *East Meets West,* London: Macmillan, 1998.

Perdue, P., *Exhausting the Earth: State and Peasant in Hunan, 1500–1850,* Cambridge, MA: Harvard University Press, 1987.

Posner, R., 'A Theory of Primitive Society, With Special Reference to Law', *Journal of Law and Economics,* 23(26), 1980.

Pye, W.L., *Chinese Negotiating Style: Commercial Approaches and Cultural Principles,* London: Quorum Books, 1992.

Redding, S.G., 'Cognition as an Aspect of Culture and Its Relation to Management Process: An Exploratory View of the Chinese Case', *Journal of Management Studies,* 17(2), 1980.

——, *The Spirit of Chinese Capitalism,* New York: Walter de Gruyter, 1990.

——, 'Culture and Business in Hong Kong' in Wang, G. and Wong, S.L., eds. *Dynamic Hong Kong: Business and Culture,* Hong Kong; Hong Kong Centre for Asian Studies, The University of Hong Kong, 1997.

—— and Tam, S., 'Networks and Molecular Organizations: An Exploratory View of Chinese Firms in Hong Kong' in Mun, K.C. and Chan, T.S., eds. *Perspectives in International Business,* Hong Kong: Chinese University Press, 1985.

Robson, A., *Civilization and the Growth of Law,* New York: Macmillan, 1935.

Schulthess, E., African rhinoceros, photograph, *Du,* Sept. 1957.

Schwartz, B., 'On Attitudes towards Law in China', in Katz, M., ed. *Government under Law and the Individual,* Washington D.C.: American Council of Learned Societies, 1957.

Scogin, H.T. Jr. 'Civil Law in Traditional China: History and Theory' in Bernhardt, K. and Huang, P.C.C., eds. *Civil Law in Qing and Republican China',* Stanford: Stanford University Press, 1994.

Scott, W.R., 'The Adolescence of Institutional Theory,' *Administrative Science Quarterly,* 32, 1987.

Silin, R.H., 'Marketing and Credit in a Hong Kong Wholesale Market' in

Willmot, W.E., ed. *Economic Organization in Chinese Society,* Stanford: Stanford University Press, 1972.

Skinner, G.W., 'Chinese Peasants and the Closed Community: An Open and Shut Case', *Comparative Studies in Society and History* 13, 3 July, 1971.

Spradley, J.P., 'Ethnography and Culture' in Worsley, P., ed. *The New Modern Sociology Readings,* England: Penguin Books, 1979/1991. Excerpted from Spradley, J.P., *The Ethnographic Interview,* New York: Holt, Rinehart and Wilson, 1979.

Swedberg, R., *Economics and Sociology: Redefining their Boundaries: Conversations with Economists and Sociologists,* Princeton: Princeton University Press, 1990.

Tai, L.S.T., 'Doing Business in the People's Republic of China', *Management International Review,* 1(8), 1988.

Terpstra, V. and David, K., *The Cultural Environment of International Business,* Cincinnati, OH: South-Western Publishing Co., 1985.

Terry, E., *The Executive Guide to China,* New York: John Wiley and Sons Inc., 1984.

Thompson, K.J., *Interdisciplinarity – History, Theory and Practice,* Detroit: Wayne State University Press, 1990.

Tolbert, P.S. and Zucker, L.G., 'The Institutionalisation of Institutional Theory', in Clegg, S.R., Hardy, C. and Nord, W.R., eds. *Handbook of Organisational Studies,* London: Sage, 1996.

Tu, I., 'Family Enterprises in Taiwan' in Hamilton, G.G., ed. *Business Networks and Economic Development in East and Southeast Asia,* Hong Kong: Hong Kong Centre of Asian Studies, University of Hong Kong, 1991.

Tylor, E.B., *Primitive Culture: Researches into the Development of Mythology, Philosophy, Religion, Language, Art and Custom,* London: J. Murray, 1903/1971.

Unger, R.M., *Law in Modern Society,* New York: The Free Press, 1976.

Van der Sprenkel, S., 'Urban Social Control' in Skinner, G.W., ed. *The City in Late Imperial China,* Stanford: Stanford University Press, 1977.

Von Neumann, J. and Morgenstern, O., *Theory of Games and Economic Behaviour,* Princeton: Princeton University Press, 1953.

Walder, A.G., *Communist Neo-Traditionalism: Work and Authority in Chinese Industry,* Berkeley, CA: University of California Press, 1986.

Wei, Zheng and Linghu, Defen, *Shui Shu,* Beijing: Zong Hua Shu Ju, 1973/1991.

Westwood, R.I., *Organization Behaviour: Southeast Asian Perspective,* Hong Kong: Longman, 1992.

Williams, R., *Keywords,* Great Britain: Fontana, 1976/1983.

Williamson, O.E., *The Economic Institutions of Capitalism,* New York: The Free Press, 1985.

——, *Industrial Organization,* England: Edward Elgar, 1990.

Winn, J.K., 'Relational Practices and the Marginalization of Law: Informal Financial Practices of Small Businesses in Taiwan', *Law and Society Review,* 28(2), 1994.

Wong, S.L., 'Chinese Entrepreneurs and Business Trust', Inaugural Lecture from the Chair of Sociology, *University of Hong Kong Supplement to the Gazette,* Vol. XXXVII No.1, 21 May 1990.

Wright, M.C., *The Last Stand of Chinese Conservatism: the Tung-Chih Restoration 1862–1874,* Stanford: Stanford University Press, 1957.

Wrong, D.H., 'The Oversocialized Conception of Man in Modern Sociology', *American Sociological Review,* 26, 1961.

Wu, J.C.H., 'Chinese Legal and Political Philosophy', in Moore, C.A., ed. *The Chinese Mind: Essentials of Chinese Philosophy and Culture,* Honolulu: East West Centre Press, 1967.

Yan, Y., *The Flow of Gifts: Reciprocity and Social Networks in a Chinese Village,* Stanford: Stanford University Press, 1996.

Yang, L., 'The Concept of *Pao* as a Basis for Social Relations in China' in Fairbank, J.K., ed. *Chinese Thought and Institutions,* Chicago: University of Chicago Press, 1957.

Yang, M.M., *Gifts, Favours and Banquets: The Art of Social Relationships in China,* Ithaca: Cornell University Press, 1994.

Yao, X., *Confucianism and Christianity: A Comparative Study of Jen and Agape,* Sussex: Sussex Academic Press, 1996.

Zhao, J., 'How should the Government Develop an Assistance Policy for Small and Medium Businesses?', *Qiyin Jikan,* 5, 1982 (Chinese publication).

Zucker, L.G., 'Organisations as Institutions', in Bacharach, S.B., ed. *Research in Sociology of Organisations,* Greenwich, CT: JAI Press, 1983.

——, 'The Role of Institutionalization in Cultural Persistence', in Powell, W.W. and DiMaggio, P.J., eds. *The New Institutionalism in Organisational Analysis,* Chicago, IL: The University of Chicago Press, 1991.

Index